All New Gifts for the Cookie Jar

♥

Lia Wilson

Cookbook Resources, LLC

All New Gifts for the Cookie Jar

1st Printing June 2005
2nd Printing December 2005
3rd Printing July 2007

Copyright © 2005
By Cookbook Resources LLC, Highland Village, Texas. All rights reserved

ISBN 1-931294-00-3

Library of Congress Number:
2005928524

Illustrated by Nancy Murphy Griffith
Edited, Designed and Published in the
United States of America and
Manufactured in China by
Cookbook Resources, LLC
541 Doubletree Drive
Highland Village, Texas 75077
Toll free 866-229-2665

www.cookbookresources.com

Table of Contents

Spectacular Gift Jars Made Easy

Use your imagination to create fun, easy and personalized gifts! This is an excellent craft project for anyone and even your little ones can help paint, glue and decorate. Gather your supplies and enjoy time together. Here are a few quick ideas and pointers:

Top It!
(Jar topper should always be secured with a rubber band.)

+ Spray paint the lid and decorate with buttons, charms, beads or old costume jewelry.
+ Cut 2 (6½ to 7-inch) (18 cm) squares of coordinating fabric. Place first square on top of the second so that the points are centered on the straight edge. The catty-corner placement produces a cute handkerchief hem and gives your friend fabric squares for her stash.
+ Use those extra blocks from former projects as lid toppers. This is a great idea for a cookie-block exchange to make gifts extra special.
+ Place jar inside a simple, fabric drawstring bag. Use novelty prints for holidays or special events.

Tie It!
(Ribbon, Wired Ribbon, Jute, Cording, Raffia or Fabric)

+ Narrow ribbon – conceal rubber band by wrapping the jar lid with several strands of narrow ribbon in the same or complimentary colors and tie in a bow. Knot each ribbon streamer a few times at different intervals for added interest.

- For a cute idea with narrow ribbon, select an antique or unique button, pull ribbon ends through the button holes and tie in a bow or knot.
- Wired ribbon or garland (stars, snowflakes, hearts, etc.) – conceal rubber band by wrapping the jar lid several times with ribbon or garland and twist to secure. Leave 6-inch (15 cm) streamers on both sides of the wire garland. Coil each end around a pencil to form a curl.

- Cording – loop small tassels around the cording for an extra touch. Be sure to knot ends of cording streamers for a great look.
- Fabric – cut fabric in 2-inch (5 cm) strips, fold lengthwise and wrap over rubber band. Tie in a bow or knot. Glue buttons, charms, beads or other embellishments as desired.

Tag It!
(Each recipe has 3 tags, which include the baking instructions.)

- Photocopy or simply cut tags from the book and attach to the jar.
- Use colored pens to add a little zip to the art already on the tag.

"Life is not measured by the breaths we take
but by the moments that take our breath away."
- Anonymous

Banana Bread Bites

Banana Bread Bites

These hearty cookies have the flavor and texture of banana bread. They make the house smell wonderful as they bake.

Ingredients for jar:

1½ cups flour	360 ml
½ teaspoon baking soda	2 ml
½ teaspoon salt	2 ml
¼ teaspoon nutmeg	1 ml
¾ teaspoon cinnamon	4 ml
1½ cups oats	360 ml
1¼ cups sugar	300 ml

Instructions for jar:

■ Sift flour with baking soda, salt, nutmeg and cinnamon.

■ Spoon into 1-quart (1 L) jar.

■ Layer oats over flour mixture then sugar over oats.

Banana Bread Bites

Instructions for baking:

¾ cup (1½ sticks) butter, softened   180 ml
1 egg, beaten
1 cup mashed bananas   240 ml
   (about 2 medium bananas)

- Preheat oven to 350° (176°C).

- Empty contents of jar into large bowl.

- Beat butter, egg and bananas.

- Add butter mixture to dry ingredients and blend well.

- Drop dough by teaspoonfuls onto sprayed baking sheet and bake for 12 to 15 minutes or until brown around edges.

- Remove from oven and cool for 1 minute before moving to cooling rack.

"The human race has one really effective weapon and that is laughter."

- Mark Twain

Banana Bread Bites

Instructions for baking:

¾ cup (1½ sticks) butter, softened	180 ml
1 egg, beaten	
1 cup mashed bananas (about 2 medium bananas)	240 ml

- Preheat oven to 350° (176°C).
- Empty contents of jar into large bowl.
- Beat butter, egg and bananas.
- Add butter mixture to dry ingredients and blend well.
- Drop dough by teaspoonfuls onto sprayed baking sheet and bake for 12 to 15 minutes or until brown around edges.
- Remove from oven and cool for 1 minute before moving to cooling rack.

- ✂

Banana Bread Bites

Instructions for baking:

¾ cup (1½ sticks) butter, softened	180 ml
1 egg, beaten	
1 cup mashed bananas (about 2 medium bananas)	240 ml

- Preheat oven to 350° (176°C).
- Empty contents of jar into large bowl.
- Beat butter, egg and bananas.
- Add butter mixture to dry ingredients and blend well.
- Drop dough by teaspoonfuls onto sprayed baking sheet and bake for 12 to 15 minutes or until brown around edges.
- Remove from oven and cool for 1 minute before moving to cooling rack.

- ✂

Banana Bread Bites

Instructions for baking:

¾ cup (1½ sticks) butter, softened	180 ml
1 egg, beaten	
1 cup mashed bananas (about 2 medium bananas)	240 ml

- Preheat oven to 350° (176°C).
- Empty contents of jar into large bowl.
- Beat butter, egg and bananas.
- Add butter mixture to dry ingredients and blend well.
- Drop dough by teaspoonfuls onto sprayed baking sheet and bake for 12 to 15 minutes or until brown around edges.
- Remove from oven and cool for 1 minute before moving to cooling rack.

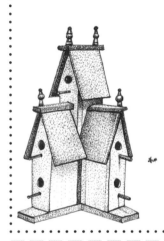

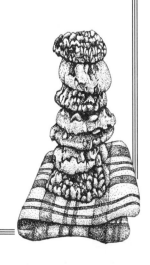

Banana Bread Bites

Instructions for baking:

¾ cup (1½ sticks) butter, softened	180 ml
1 egg, beaten	
1 cup mashed bananas (about 2 medium bananas)	240 ml

- Preheat oven to 350° (176°C).
- Empty contents of jar into large bowl.
- Beat butter, egg and bananas.
- Add butter mixture to dry ingredients and blend well.
- Drop dough by teaspoonfuls onto sprayed baking sheet and bake for 12 to 15 minutes or until brown around edges.
- Remove from oven and cool for 1 minute before moving to cooling rack.

Banana Bread Bites

Instructions for baking:

¾ cup (1½ sticks) butter, softened	180 ml
1 egg, beaten	
1 cup mashed bananas (about 2 medium bananas)	240 ml

- Preheat oven to 350° (176°C).
- Empty contents of jar into large bowl.
- Beat butter, egg and bananas.
- Add butter mixture to dry ingredients and blend well.
- Drop dough by teaspoonfuls onto sprayed baking sheet and bake for 12 to 15 minutes or until brown around edges.
- Remove from oven and cool for 1 minute before moving to cooling rack.

Banana Bread Bites

Instructions for baking:

¾ cup (1½ sticks) butter, softened	180 ml
1 egg, beaten	
1 cup mashed bananas (about 2 medium bananas)	240 ml

- Preheat oven to 350° (176°C).
- Empty contents of jar into large bowl.
- Beat butter, egg and bananas.
- Add butter mixture to dry ingredients and blend well.
- Drop dough by teaspoonfuls onto sprayed baking sheet and bake for 12 to 15 minutes or until brown around edges.
- Remove from oven and cool for 1 minute before moving to cooling rack.

Iced Buttery Orange Cookies

Iced Buttery Orange Cookies

Ingredients for jar:

1 cup sugar	240 ml
1 cup coarsely chopped walnuts or pecans	240 ml
2 cups flour	480 ml
½ teaspoon baking powder	2 ml
½ teaspoon salt	2 ml
2 tablespoons dried orange peel	30 ml

Instructions for jar:

■ Spoon sugar into 1-quart (1 L) jar.

■ Sprinkle chopped nuts over sugar.

■ Combine flour with baking powder, salt and orange peel.

■ Spoon flour mixture over chopped nuts.

♥ *Decorate jar using the suggestions and tips found on pages 4 and 5.*

Iced Buttery Orange Cookies

Instructions for baking:

1 cup (2 sticks) butter, softened   **240 ml**
1 egg, beaten

- Preheat oven to 350° (176°C).

- Empty contents of jar into large mixing bowl.

- Stir butter and egg into dry ingredients until dough is mixed well.

- Drop dough by rounded teaspoonfuls on ungreased baking sheet.

- Bake 9 to 11 minutes or until edges are light brown.

- Cool and ice, if desired, before storing.

Icing Recipe (optional):

1 cup powdered sugar   **240 ml**
2 tablespoons orange juice   **30 ml**

- Add enough orange juice, a little at a time, to powdered sugar and stir as you add it, until it reaches frosting consistency.

- Drizzle icing over cookies and let dry.

Iced Buttery Orange Cookies

Instructions for baking:

1 cup (2 sticks) butter, softened	240 ml
1 egg, beaten	

- Preheat oven to 350° (176°C).
- Empty contents of jar into large mixing bowl.
- Stir butter and egg into dry ingredients and mix well.
- Drop dough by rounded teaspoonfuls on ungreased baking sheet.
- Bake for 9 to 11 minutes or until edges are light brown.
- Cool and ice, if desired, before storing.

Icing Recipe (optional):

1 cup powdered sugar	240 ml
2 tablespoons orange juice	30 ml

- Add enough orange juice, a little at a time, to powdered sugar and stir until you reach frosting consistency.
- Drizzle icing over cookies and let dry.

Iced Buttery Orange Cookies

Instructions for baking:

1 cup (2 sticks) butter, softened	240 ml
1 egg, beaten	

- Preheat oven to 350° (176°C).
- Empty contents of jar into large mixing bowl.
- Stir butter and egg into dry ingredients and mix well.
- Drop dough by rounded teaspoonfuls on ungreased baking sheet.
- Bake for 9 to 11 minutes or until edges are light brown.
- Cool and ice, if desired, before storing.

Icing Recipe (optional):

1 cup powdered sugar	240 ml
2 tablespoons orange juice	30 ml

- Add enough orange juice, a little at a time, to powdered sugar and stir until you reach frosting consistency.
- Drizzle icing over cookies and let dry.

www.cookbookresources.com

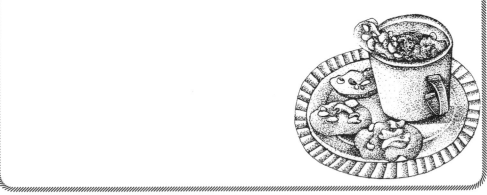

Iced Buttery Orange Cookies

Instructions for baking:

1 cup (2 sticks) butter, softened	240 ml
1 egg, beaten	

- Preheat oven to 350° (176°C).
- Empty contents of jar into large mixing bowl.
- Stir butter and egg into dry ingredients and mix well.
- Drop dough by rounded teaspoonfuls on ungreased baking sheet.
- Bake for 9 to 11 minutes or until edges are light brown.
- Cool and ice, if desired, before storing.

Icing Recipe (optional):

1 cup powdered sugar	240 ml
2 tablespoons orange juice	30 ml

- Add enough orange juice, a little at a time, to powdered sugar and stir until you reach frosting consistency.
- Drizzle icing over cookies and let dry.

www.cookbookresources.com

- ✂

Iced Buttery Orange Cookies

Instructions for baking:

1 cup (2 sticks) butter, softened	240 ml
1 egg, beaten	

- Preheat oven to 350° (176°C).
- Empty contents of jar into large mixing bowl.
- Stir butter and egg into dry ingredients and mix well.
- Drop dough by rounded teaspoonfuls on ungreased baking sheet.
- Bake for 9 to 11 minutes or until edges are light brown.
- Cool and ice, if desired, before storing.

Icing Recipe (optional):

1 cup powdered sugar	240 ml
2 tablespoons orange juice	30 ml

- Add enough orange juice, a little at a time, to powdered sugar and stir until you reach frosting consistency.
- Drizzle icing over cookies and let dry.

www.cookbookresources.com

Iced Pineapple Cookies

Iced Pineapple Cookies

These pineapple cookies have a cake-like texture.
The icing adds a special touch and added flavor.

Ingredients for jar:

½ cup sugar	120 ml
½ cup packed brown sugar	120 ml
2 cups flour	480 ml
½ teaspoon baking powder	2 ml
½ cup chopped pecans	120 ml
½ cup shredded coconut	120 ml

Instructions for jar:

- Spoon sugar into 1-quart (1 L) jar.

- Spoon brown sugar over sugar.

- Combine flour with baking powder and spoon over brown sugar.

- Layer pecans over flour mixture and coconut over pecans.

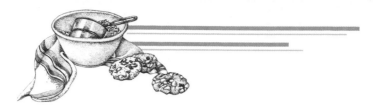

Iced Pineapple Cookies

Instructions for baking:

1 egg	
1 (8 ounce) can crushed pineapple, with juice	227 g
1 teaspoon vanilla	5 ml
½ cup (1 stick) butter, softened	120 ml

- Preheat oven to 350° (176° C).

- Empty contents of jar into large mixing bowl and stir to combine ingredients. Drain pineapple juice and save.

- In small bowl, whisk egg, pineapple and vanilla. Add egg mixture to dry ingredients and stir well.

- Drop dough by teaspoonfuls on sprayed baking sheet and bake for 12 to 14 minutes.

- Remove from oven and transfer to cooling rack. If desired, use reserved juice in icing recipe and frost when cool.

Pineapple Icing (optional):

1 cup powdered sugar	240 ml
½ cup (1 stick) butter, softened	120 ml
2 tablespoons pineapple juice	30 ml

- Combine sugar and butter in small mixing bowl.

- Add enough reserved pineapple juice to reach spreading consistency.

- Frost when cool.

Iced Pineapple Cookies

Instructions for baking:

1 egg	
1 (8 ounce) can crushed pineapple, with juice	**227 g**
1 teaspoon vanilla	**5 ml**
½ cup (1 stick) butter, softened	**120 ml**

- Preheat oven to 350°(176° C).
- Empty contents of jar into large mixing bowl and stir to combine ingredients. Drain pineapple juice and save.
- In small bowl, whisk egg, pineapple and vanilla. Add egg mixture to dry ingredients and stir well.
- Drop dough by teaspoonfuls on sprayed baking sheet and bake for 12 to 14 minutes.
- Remove from oven and transfer to cooling rack. If desired, use reserved juice in icing recipe and frost when cool.

Pineapple Icing (optional):

1 cup powdered sugar	**240 ml**
½ cup (1 stick) butter, softened	**120 ml**
2 tablespoons pineapple juice	**30 ml**

- Combine sugar and butter in small mixing bowl.
- Add enough reserved pineapple juice to reach spreading consistency.
- Frost when cool.

- ✂

Iced Pineapple Cookies

Instructions for baking:

1 egg	
1 (8 ounce) can crushed pineapple, with juice	**227 g**
1 teaspoon vanilla	**5 ml**
½ cup (1 stick) butter, softened	**120 ml**

- Preheat oven to 350°(176° C).
- Empty contents of jar into large mixing bowl and stir to combine ingredients. Drain pineapple juice and save.
- In small bowl, whisk egg, pineapple and vanilla. Add egg mixture to dry ingredients and stir well.
- Drop dough by teaspoonfuls on sprayed baking sheet and bake for 12 to 14 minutes.
- Remove from oven and transfer to cooling rack. If desired, use reserved juice in icing recipe and frost when cool.

Pineapple Icing (optional):

1 cup powdered sugar	**240 ml**
½ cup (1 stick) butter, softened	**120 ml**
2 tablespoons pineapple juice	**30 ml**

- Combine sugar and butter in small mixing bowl.
- Add enough reserved pineapple juice to reach spreading consistency.
- Frost when cool.

www.cookbookresources.com

Iced Pineapple Cookies

Instructions for baking:

1 egg	
1 (8 ounce) can crushed pineapple, with juice	**227 g**
1 teaspoon vanilla	**5 ml**
½ cup (1 stick) butter, softened	**120 ml**

- Preheat oven to 350°(176° C).
- Empty contents of jar into large mixing bowl and stir to combine ingredients. Drain pineapple juice and save.
- In small bowl, whisk egg, pineapple and vanilla. Add egg mixture to dry ingredients and stir well.
- Drop dough by teaspoonfuls on sprayed baking sheet and bake for 12 to 14 minutes.
- Remove from oven and transfer to cooling rack. If desired, use reserved juice in icing recipe and frost when cool.

Pineapple Icing (optional):

1 cup powdered sugar	**240 ml**
½ cup (1 stick) butter, softened	**120 ml**
2 tablespoons pineapple juice	**30 ml**

- Combine sugar and butter in small mixing bowl.
- Add enough reserved pineapple juice to reach spreading consistency.
- Frost when cool.

www.cookbookresources.com

Iced Pineapple Cookies

Instructions for baking:

1 egg	
1 (8 ounce) can crushed pineapple, with juice	**227 g**
1 teaspoon vanilla	**5 ml**
½ cup (1 stick) butter, softened	**120 ml**

- Preheat oven to 350°(176° C).
- Empty contents of jar into large mixing bowl and stir to combine ingredients. Drain pineapple juice and save.
- In small bowl, whisk egg, pineapple and vanilla. Add egg mixture to dry ingredients and stir well.
- Drop dough by teaspoonfuls on sprayed baking sheet and bake for 12 to 14 minutes.
- Remove from oven and transfer to cooling rack. If desired, use reserved juice in icing recipe and frost when cool.

Pineapple Icing (optional):

1 cup powdered sugar	**240 ml**
½ cup (1 stick) butter, softened	**120 ml**
2 tablespoons pineapple juice	**30 ml**

- Combine sugar and butter in small mixing bowl.
- Add enough reserved pineapple juice to reach spreading consistency.
- Frost when cool.

www.cookbookresources.com

Mint Chocolate Cookies

Mint Chocolate Cookies

Ingredients for jar:

¾ cup sugar	180 ml
1 cup packed brown sugar	240 ml
1¾ cups flour	420 ml
1 teaspoon baking soda	5 ml
½ teaspoon salt	2 ml
¼ cup cocoa	60 ml
½ cup mint chocolate chips	120 ml

Instructions for jar:

- Place sugar in 1-quart (1 L) jar and spoon brown sugar over sugar.

- Combine flour, baking soda and salt. Spoon mixture over brown sugar.

- Spoon cocoa over flour mixture, add chocolate chips on top and press gently to fit.

Mint Chocolate Cookies

Instructions for baking:

1 cup (2 sticks) butter, softened	**240 ml**
1 teaspoon vanilla	**5 ml**
1 egg	

■ Preheat oven to 350° (176° C).

■ Empty contents of jar into large bowl.

■ Beat egg with vanilla and butter.

■ Add egg mixture to dry ingredients in bowl and stir well.

■ Drop by teaspoonfuls on ungreased baking sheet.

■ Bake for 7 to 10 minutes.

"*A friend is one to whom one may pour out all the contents of one's heart, chaff and grain together, knowing that the gentlest of hands will take and sift it, keep what is worth keeping and with a breath of kindness blow the rest away.*"

- Arabian Proverb

Mint Chocolate Cookies

Instructions for baking:

1 cup (2 sticks) butter, softened	**240 ml**
1 teaspoon vanilla	**5 ml**
1 egg	

- Preheat oven to 350° (176° C).
- Empty contents of jar into large bowl.
- Beat egg with vanilla and butter.
- Add egg mixture to dry ingredients in bowl and stir well.
- Drop by teaspoonfuls on ungreased baking sheet.
- Bake for 7 to 10 minutes.

Mint Chocolate Cookies

Instructions for baking:

1 cup (2 sticks) butter, softened	**240 ml**
1 teaspoon vanilla	**5 ml**
1 egg	

- Preheat oven to 350° (176° C).
- Empty contents of jar into large bowl.
- Beat egg with vanilla and butter.
- Add egg mixture to dry ingredients in bowl and stir well.
- Drop by teaspoonfuls on ungreased baking sheet.
- Bake for 7 to 10 minutes.

Mint Chocolate Cookies

Instructions for baking:

1 cup (2 sticks) butter, softened	**240 ml**
1 teaspoon vanilla	**5 ml**
1 egg	

- Preheat oven to 350° (176° C).
- Empty contents of jar into large bowl.
- Beat egg with vanilla and butter.
- Add egg mixture to dry ingredients in bowl and stir well.
- Drop by teaspoonfuls on ungreased baking sheet.
- Bake for 7 to 10 minutes.

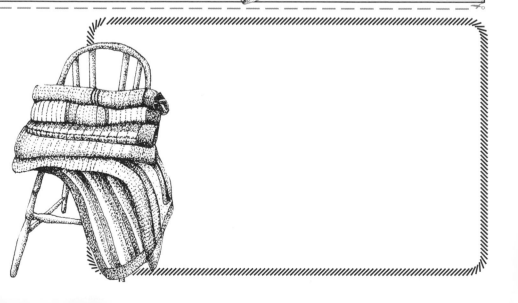

Mint Chocolate Cookies

Instructions for baking:

1 cup (2 sticks) butter, softened   **240 ml**
1 teaspoon vanilla   **5 ml**
1 egg

- Preheat oven to 350° (176° C).
- Empty contents of jar into large bowl.
- Beat egg with vanilla and butter.
- Add egg mixture to dry ingredients in bowl and stir well.
- Drop by teaspoonfuls on ungreased baking sheet.
- Bake for 7 to 10 minutes.

Mint Chocolate Cookies

Instructions for baking:

1 cup (2 sticks) butter, softened   **240 ml**
1 teaspoon vanilla   **5 ml**
1 egg

- Preheat oven to 350° (176° C).
- Empty contents of jar into large bowl.
- Beat egg with vanilla and butter.
- Add egg mixture to dry ingredients in bowl and stir well.
- Drop by teaspoonfuls on ungreased baking sheet.
- Bake for 7 to 10 minutes.

Mint Chocolate Cookies

Instructions for baking:

1 cup (2 sticks) butter, softened   **240 ml**
1 teaspoon vanilla   **5 ml**
1 egg

- Preheat oven to 350° (176° C).
- Empty contents of jar into large bowl.
- Beat egg with vanilla and butter.
- Add egg mixture to dry ingredients in bowl and stir well.
- Drop by teaspoonfuls on ungreased baking sheet.
- Bake for 7 to 10 minutes.

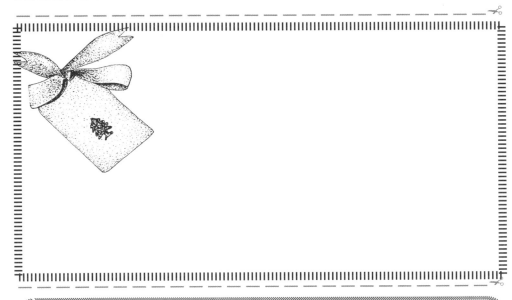

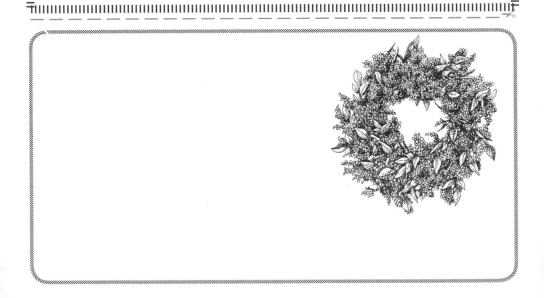

Crispy Cracklin' Cookies

Crispy Cracklin' Cookies

Ingredients for jar:

½ cup sugar	120 ml
½ cup packed brown sugar	120 ml
1 cup flour	240 ml
½ teaspoon baking soda	2 ml
½ teaspoon baking powder	2 ml
½ teaspoon salt	2 ml
1 cup quick-cooking oats	240 ml
1¼ cups crisped rice cereal	300 ml

Instructions for jar:

■ Put sugar in 1-quart (1 L) jar.

■ Layer brown sugar over sugar.

■ Combine flour, baking soda, baking powder and salt. Spoon over brown sugar.

■ Layer oats over flour mixture and cereal over oats.

♥ *Decorate jar using the suggestions and tips found on pages 4 and 5.*

Crispy Cracklin' Cookies

Ingredients for baking:

½ cup (1 stick) butter, softened   **120 ml**
1 egg
1 teaspoon vanilla   **5 ml**

- Preheat oven to 350° (176° C).

- Whisk butter, egg, and vanilla in large mixing bowl.

- Empty cookie mix from jar into medium mixing bowl and stir to combine ingredients.

- Slowly add dry cookie mixture to egg mixture and stir after each addition.

- Drop dough by teaspoonfuls on lightly sprayed baking sheet.

- Bake for 8 to 10 minutes or until cookies are light brown.

" *Let us be grateful to people who make us happy; they are the charming gardeners who make our souls blossom.*"
- *Marcel Proust*

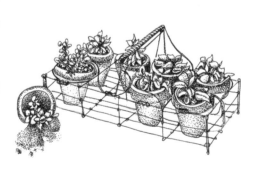

Crispy Cracklin' Cookies

Instructions for baking:

½ cup (1 stick) butter, softened	120 ml
1 egg	
1 teaspoon vanilla	5 ml

- Preheat oven to 350° (176° C).
- Whisk butter, egg, and vanilla in large mixing bowl.
- Empty cookie mix from jar into medium mixing bowl and stir to combine ingredients.
- Slowly add dry cookie mixture to egg mixture and stir after each addition.
- Drop dough by teaspoonfuls on lightly sprayed baking sheet.
- Bake for 8 to 10 minutes or until cookies are light brown.

www.cookbookresources.com

Crispy Cracklin' Cookies

Instructions for baking:

½ cup (1 stick) butter, softened	120 ml
1 egg	
1 teaspoon vanilla	5 ml

- Preheat oven to 350° (176° C).
- Whisk butter, egg, and vanilla in large mixing bowl.
- Empty cookie mix from jar into medium mixing bowl and stir to combine ingredients.
- Slowly add dry cookie mixture to egg mixture and stir after each addition.
- Drop dough by teaspoonfuls on lightly sprayed baking sheet.
- Bake for 8 to 10 minutes or until cookies are light brown.

www.cookbookresources.com

Crispy Cracklin' Cookies

Instructions for baking:

½ cup (1 stick) butter, softened	120 ml
1 egg	
1 teaspoon vanilla	5 ml

- Preheat oven to 350° (176° C).
- Whisk butter, egg, and vanilla in large mixing bowl.
- Empty cookie mix from jar into medium mixing bowl and stir to combine ingredients.
- Slowly add dry cookie mixture to egg mixture and stir after each addition.
- Drop dough by teaspoonfuls on lightly sprayed baking sheet.
- Bake for 8 to 10 minutes or until cookies are light brown.

www.cookbookresources.com

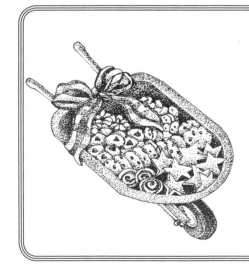

Crispy Cracklin' Cookies

Instructions for baking:

½ cup (1 stick) butter, softened	120 ml
1 egg	
1 teaspoon vanilla	5 ml

- Preheat oven to 350° (176° C).
- Whisk butter, egg, and vanilla in large mixing bowl.
- Empty cookie mix from jar into medium mixing bowl and stir to combine ingredients.
- Slowly add dry cookie mixture to egg mixture and stir after each addition.
- Drop dough by teaspoonfuls on lightly sprayed baking sheet.
- Bake for 8 to 10 minutes or until cookies are light brown.

www.cookbookresources.com

- ✂

Crispy Cracklin' Cookies

Instructions for baking:

½ cup (1 stick) butter, softened	120 ml
1 egg	
1 teaspoon vanilla	5 ml

- Preheat oven to 350° (176° C).
- Whisk butter, egg, and vanilla in large mixing bowl.
- Empty cookie mix from jar into medium mixing bowl and stir to combine ingredients.
- Slowly add dry cookie mixture to egg mixture and stir after each addition.
- Drop dough by teaspoonfuls on lightly sprayed baking sheet.
- Bake for 8 to 10 minutes or until cookies are light brown.

www.cookbookresources.com

- ✂

Crispy Cracklin' Cookies

Instructions for baking:

½ cup (1 stick) butter, softened	120 ml
1 egg	
1 teaspoon vanilla	5 ml

- Preheat oven to 350° (176° C).
- Whisk butter, egg, and vanilla in large mixing bowl.
- Empty cookie mix from jar into medium mixing bowl and stir to combine ingredients.
- Slowly add dry cookie mixture to egg mixture and stir after each addition.
- Drop dough by teaspoonfuls on lightly sprayed baking sheet.
- Bake for 8 to 10 minutes or until cookies are light brown.

www.cookbookresources.com

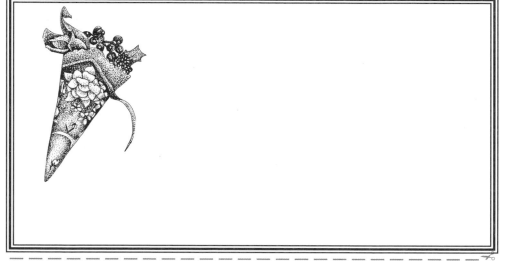

Dark, Rich Walnut Cookies

Dark, Rich Walnut Cookies

*These dark cookies have a deep caramel flavor.
They're crisp on the outside and chewy on the inside.*

Ingredients for jar:

1½ cups packed dark brown sugar	360 ml
2½ cups flour	600 ml
¼ cup finely chopped walnuts	60 ml

Instructions for jar:

- Pack brown sugar in bottom of 1-quart (1 L) jar.

- Spoon flour over brown sugar.

- Place walnuts over flour.

♥ *Decorate jar using the suggestions and tips found on pages 4 and 5.*

Dark, Rich Walnut Cookies

Instructions for baking:

1 cup (2 sticks) butter, softened	**240 ml**
1 egg yolk	
1 tablespoon vanilla	**15 ml**
¼ cup sugar	**60 ml**

- Preheat oven to 350° (176°C).

- Empty contents of jar into large mixing bowl. Stir to mix ingredients.

- Beat butter with egg yolk and vanilla.

- Add egg mixture to dry ingredients in bowl and mix well.

- Shape dough into 1-inch (2.5) cm balls and chill for 2 to 3 hours.

- Place chilled dough balls on ungreased baking sheet and flatten each one slightly with bottom of glass dipped in sugar.

- Bake for 12 to 13 minutes.

"*But friendship is precious, not only in the shade, but in the sunshine of life; and thanks to a benevolent arrangement of things, the greater part of life is sunshine.*"
- *Thomas Jefferson*

Dark, Rich Walnut Cookies

Instructions for baking:

1 cup (2 sticks) butter, softened	240 ml
1 egg yolk	
1 tablespoon vanilla	15 ml
¼ cup sugar	60 ml

- Preheat oven to 350° (176°C).
- Empty contents of jar into large mixing bowl. Stir to mix ingredients.
- Beat butter with egg yolk and vanilla.
- Add egg mixture to dry ingredients in bowl and mix well.
- Shape dough into 1-inch (2.5 cm) balls and chill for 2 to 3 hours.
- Place chilled dough balls on ungreased baking sheet and flatten each one slightly with bottom of glass dipped in sugar.
- Bake for 12 to 13 minutes.

www.cookbookresources.com

- ✂

Dark, Rich Walnut Cookies

Instructions for baking:

1 cup (2 sticks) butter, softened	240 ml
1 egg yolk	
1 tablespoon vanilla	15 ml
¼ cup sugar	60 ml

- Preheat oven to 350° (176°C).
- Empty contents of jar into large mixing bowl. Stir to mix ingredients.
- Beat butter with egg yolk and vanilla.
- Add egg mixture to dry ingredients in bowl and mix well.
- Shape dough into 1-inch (2.5 cm) balls and chill for 2 to 3 hours.
- Place chilled dough balls on ungreased baking sheet and flatten each one slightly with bottom of glass dipped in sugar.
- Bake for 12 to 13 minutes.

www.cookbookresources.com

- ✂

Dark, Rich Walnut Cookies

Instructions for baking:

1 cup (2 sticks) butter, softened	240 ml
1 egg yolk	
1 tablespoon vanilla	15 ml
¼ cup sugar	60 ml

- Preheat oven to 350° (176°C).
- Empty contents of jar into large mixing bowl. Stir to mix ingredients.
- Beat butter with egg yolk and vanilla.
- Add egg mixture to dry ingredients in bowl and mix well.
- Shape dough into 1-inch (2.5 cm) balls and chill for 2 to 3 hours.
- Place chilled dough balls on ungreased baking sheet and flatten each one slightly with bottom of glass dipped in sugar.
- Bake for 12 to 13 minutes.

www.cookbookresources.com

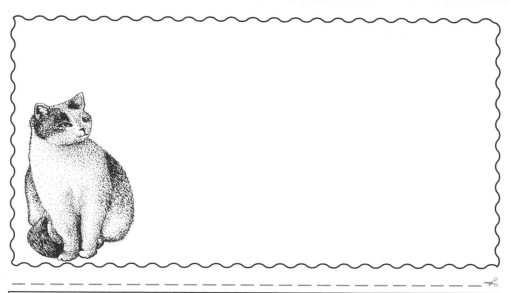

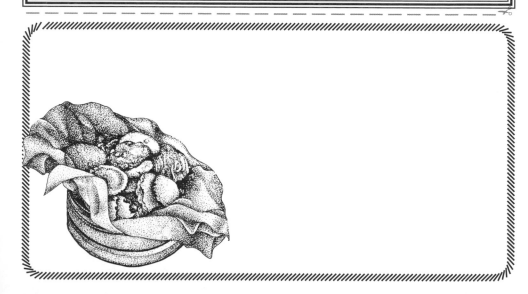

Dark, Rich Walnut Cookies

Instructions for baking:

1 cup (2 sticks) butter, softened	240 ml
1 egg yolk	
1 tablespoon vanilla	15 ml
¼ cup sugar	60 ml

- Preheat oven to 350° (176°C).
- Empty contents of jar into large mixing bowl. Stir to mix ingredients.
- Beat butter with egg yolk and vanilla.
- Add egg mixture to dry ingredients in bowl and mix well.
- Shape dough into 1-inch (2.5 cm) balls and chill for 2 to 3 hours.
- Place chilled dough balls on ungreased baking sheet and flatten each one slightly with bottom of glass dipped in sugar.
- Bake for 12 to 13 minutes.

www.cookbookresources.com

Dark, Rich Walnut Cookies

Instructions for baking:

1 cup (2 sticks) butter, softened	240 ml
1 egg yolk	
1 tablespoon vanilla	15 ml
¼ cup sugar	60 ml

- Preheat oven to 350° (176°C).
- Empty contents of jar into large mixing bowl. Stir to mix ingredients.
- Beat butter with egg yolk and vanilla.
- Add egg mixture to dry ingredients in bowl and mix well.
- Shape dough into 1-inch (2.5 cm) balls and chill for 2 to 3 hours.
- Place chilled dough balls on ungreased baking sheet and flatten each one slightly with bottom of glass dipped in sugar.
- Bake for 12 to 13 minutes.

www.cookbookresources.com

Dark, Rich Walnut Cookies

Instructions for baking:

1 cup (2 sticks) butter, softened	240 ml
1 egg yolk	
1 tablespoon vanilla	15 ml
¼ cup sugar	60 ml

- Preheat oven to 350° (176°C).
- Empty contents of jar into large mixing bowl. Stir to mix ingredients.
- Beat butter with egg yolk and vanilla.
- Add egg mixture to dry ingredients in bowl and mix well.
- Shape dough into 1-inch (2.5 cm) balls and chill for 2 to 3 hours.
- Place chilled dough balls on ungreased baking sheet and flatten each one slightly with bottom of glass dipped in sugar.
- Bake for 12 to 13 minutes.

www.cookbookresources.com

Pecan Slices

Pecan Slices

This is a cookie for the pecan lover. It's a sweet, chewy cookie bursting with pecan flavor. It's also very attractive. The cookies are sliced from a roll and each one is nicely round and the same size.

Ingredients for jar:

1 cup sugar	240 ml
¼ cup packed brown sugar	60 ml
2 cups flour	480 ml
2 teaspoons baking powder	10 ml
¼ teaspoon salt	1 ml
1 cup finely chopped pecans	240 ml

Instructions for jar:

- Spoon sugar into 1 quart (1 l) jar.

- Spoon brown sugar over sugar.

- Combine flour, baking powder and salt. Spoon over brown sugar.

- Layer pecans over flour mixture.

♥ *Decorate jar using the suggestions and tips found on pages 4 and 5.*

Pecan Slices

Instructions for baking:

1 cup (2 sticks) butter, melted	**240 ml**
1 egg	
1½ teaspoons vanilla	**7 ml**

- Empty contents of jar into large mixing bowl.

- In another bowl, combine butter, egg and vanilla and mix well.

- Stir egg mixture into dry ingredients.

- Divide dough in half and shape each half into log 3 inches (8 cm) wide.

- Wrap dough in wax paper and chill for several hours.

- To bake, preheat oven to 350° (176°C). Cut dough into ¼-inch (.6) cm slices and place on ungreased baking sheet.

- Bake for 12 to 15 minutes or until cookies are light brown.

" *How far you go in life depends on your being tender with the young, compassionate with the aged, sympathetic with the striving and tolerant with the weak and strong. Because someday in life you will have been all of these.*"
- *George Washington Carver*

Pecan Slices

Instructions for baking:

1 cup (2 sticks) butter, melted	240 ml
1 egg	
1½ teaspoons vanilla	7 ml

- Empty contents of jar into large mixing bowl.
- In another bowl, combine butter, egg and vanilla and mix well.
- Stir egg mixture into dry ingredients.
- Divide dough in half and shape each half into log 3 inches (8 cm) wide.
- Wrap dough in wax paper and chill for several hours.
- To bake, preheat oven to 350° (176°C). Cut dough into ¼-inch (.6 cm) slices and place on ungreased baking sheet.
- Bake for 12 to 15 minutes or until cookies are light brown.

www.cookbookresources.com

- ✂

Pecan Slices

Instructions for baking:

1 cup (2 sticks) butter, melted	240 ml
1 egg	
1½ teaspoons vanilla	7 ml

- Empty contents of jar into large mixing bowl.
- In another bowl, combine butter, egg and vanilla and mix well.
- Stir egg mixture into dry ingredients.
- Divide dough in half and shape each half into log 3 inches (8 cm) wide.
- Wrap dough in wax paper and chill for several hours.
- To bake, preheat oven to 350° (176°C). Cut dough into ¼-inch (.6 cm) slices and place on ungreased baking sheet.
- Bake for 12 to 15 minutes or until cookies are light brown.

www.cookbookresources.com

- ✂

Pecan Slices

Instructions for baking:

1 cup (2 sticks) butter, melted	240 ml
1 egg	
1½ teaspoons vanilla	7 ml

- Empty contents of jar into large mixing bowl.
- In another bowl, combine butter, egg and vanilla and mix well.
- Stir egg mixture into dry ingredients.
- Divide dough in half and shape each half into log 3 inches (8 cm) wide.
- Wrap dough in wax paper and chill for several hours.
- To bake, preheat oven to 350° (176°C). Cut dough into ¼-inch (.6 cm) slices and place on ungreased baking sheet.
- Bake for 12 to 15 minutes or until cookies are light brown.

www.cookbookresources.com

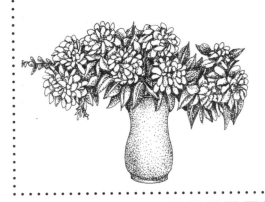

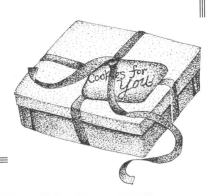

Pecan Slices

Instructions for baking:

1 cup (2 sticks) butter, melted	**240 ml**
1 egg	
1½ teaspoons vanilla	**7 ml**

- Empty contents of jar into large mixing bowl.
- In another bowl, combine butter, egg and vanilla and mix well.
- Stir egg mixture into dry ingredients.
- Divide dough in half and shape each half into log 3 inches (8 cm) wide.
- Wrap dough in wax paper and chill for several hours.
- To bake, preheat oven to 350° (176°C). Cut dough into ¼-inch (.6 cm) slices and place on ungreased baking sheet.
- Bake for 12 to 15 minutes or until cookies are light brown.

www.cookbookresources.com

Pecan Slices

Instructions for baking:

1 cup (2 sticks) butter, melted	**240 ml**
1 egg	
1½ teaspoons vanilla	**7 ml**

- Empty contents of jar into large mixing bowl.
- In another bowl, combine butter, egg and vanilla and mix well.
- Stir egg mixture into dry ingredients.
- Divide dough in half and shape each half into log 3 inches (8 cm) wide.
- Wrap dough in wax paper and chill for several hours.
- To bake, preheat oven to 350° (176°C). Cut dough into ¼-inch (.6 cm) slices and place on ungreased baking sheet.
- Bake for 12 to 15 minutes or until cookies are light brown.

www.cookbookresources.com

Pecan Slices

Instructions for baking:

1 cup (2 sticks) butter, melted	**240 ml**
1 egg	
1½ teaspoons vanilla	**7 ml**

- Empty contents of jar into large mixing bowl.
- In another bowl, combine butter, egg and vanilla and mix well.
- Stir egg mixture into dry ingredients.
- Divide dough in half and shape each half into log 3 inches (8 cm) wide.
- Wrap dough in wax paper and chill for several hours.
- To bake, preheat oven to 350° (176°C). Cut dough into ¼-inch (.6 cm) slices and place on ungreased baking sheet.
- Bake for 12 to 15 minutes or until cookies are light brown.

www.cookbookresources.com

Sesame Cookies

Sesame Cookies

Ingredients for jar:

2 cups flour	480 ml
1 teaspoon baking powder	5 ml
½ teaspoon baking soda	2 ml
½ teaspoon salt	2 ml
¾ cup sesame seeds	180 ml
1 cup packed brown sugar	240 ml
½ cup sugar	120 ml

Instructions for jar:

- Combine flour with baking powder, baking soda and salt. Spoon mixture into 1-quart (1 L) jar.

- Spread sesame seeds on baking sheet and brown lightly at 300° (148°C).

- Spoon toasted sesame seeds over flour.

- Layer brown sugar, and then sugar, over sesame seeds.

♥ *Decorate jar using the suggestions and tips found on pages 4 and 5.*

Sesame Cookies

Instructions for baking:

¾ cup (1½ sticks) butter, softened	**180 ml**
1 egg	
1 teaspoon vanilla	**5 ml**

- Preheat oven to 350° (176°C).

- Empty contents of jar into large bowl and stir to mix.

- In small bowl, whisk butter with egg and vanilla.

- Add butter mixture to dry ingredients and stir well.

- Scoop teaspoonfuls of dough and roll into balls.

- Place balls on sprayed baking sheet and flatten with fork.

- Bake for 8 to 10 minutes.

"Walking with a friend in the dark is better than walking alone in the light."

- Helen Keller

Sesame Cookies

Instructions for baking:

¾ cup (1½ sticks) butter, softened	180 ml
1 egg	
1 teaspoon vanilla	5 ml

- Preheat oven to 350° (176°C).
- Empty contents of jar into large bowl and stir to mix.
- In small bowl, whisk butter with egg and vanilla.
- Add butter mixture to dry ingredients and stir well.
- Scoop teaspoonfuls of dough and roll into balls.
- Place balls on sprayed baking sheet and flatten with fork.
- Bake for 8 to 10 minutes.

www.cookbookresources.com

Sesame Cookies

Instructions for baking:

¾ cup (1½ sticks) butter, softened	180 ml
1 egg	
1 teaspoon vanilla	5 ml

- Preheat oven to 350° (176°C).
- Empty contents of jar into large bowl and stir to mix.
- In small bowl, whisk butter with egg and vanilla.
- Add butter mixture to dry ingredients and stir well.
- Scoop teaspoonfuls of dough and roll into balls.
- Place balls on sprayed baking sheet and flatten with fork.
- Bake for 8 to 10 minutes.

www.cookbookresources.com

Sesame Cookies

Instructions for baking:

¾ cup (1½ sticks) butter, softened	180 ml
1 egg	
1 teaspoon vanilla	5 ml

- Preheat oven to 350° (176°C).
- Empty contents of jar into large bowl and stir to mix.
- In small bowl, whisk butter with egg and vanilla.
- Add butter mixture to dry ingredients and stir well.
- Scoop teaspoonfuls of dough and roll into balls.
- Place balls on sprayed baking sheet and flatten with fork.
- Bake for 8 to 10 minutes.

www.cookbookresources.com

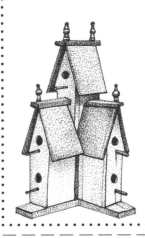

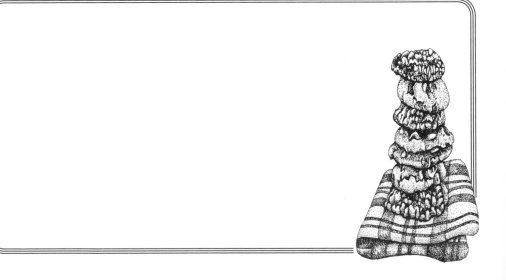

Sesame Cookies

Instructions for baking:

¾ cup (1½ sticks) butter, softened	180 ml
1 egg	
1 teaspoon vanilla	5 ml

- Preheat oven to 350° (176°C).
- Empty contents of jar into large bowl and stir to mix.
- In small bowl, whisk butter with egg and vanilla.
- Add butter mixture to dry ingredients and stir well.
- Scoop teaspoonfuls of dough and roll into balls.
- Place balls on sprayed baking sheet and flatten with fork.
- Bake for 8 to 10 minutes.

Sesame Cookies

Instructions for baking:

¾ cup (1½ sticks) butter, softened	180 ml
1 egg	
1 teaspoon vanilla	5 ml

- Preheat oven to 350° (176°C).
- Empty contents of jar into large bowl and stir to mix.
- In small bowl, whisk butter with egg and vanilla.
- Add butter mixture to dry ingredients and stir well.
- Scoop teaspoonfuls of dough and roll into balls.
- Place balls on sprayed baking sheet and flatten with fork.
- Bake for 8 to 10 minutes.

www.cookbookresources.com

Sesame Cookies

Instructions for baking:

¾ cup (1½ sticks) butter, softened	180 ml
1 egg	
1 teaspoon vanilla	5 ml

- Preheat oven to 350° (176°C).
- Empty contents of jar into large bowl and stir to mix.
- In small bowl, whisk butter with egg and vanilla.
- Add butter mixture to dry ingredients and stir well.
- Scoop teaspoonfuls of dough and roll into balls.
- Place balls on sprayed baking sheet and flatten with fork.
- Bake for 8 to 10 minutes.

www.cookbookresources.com

Crisp Coconut Cookies

Crisp Coconut Cookies

Ingredients for jar:

½ cup sugar	120 ml
½ cup packed brown sugar	120 ml
1 cup flour	240 ml
½ teaspoon baking powder	2 ml
½ teaspoon baking soda	2 ml
½ teaspoon salt	2 ml
1 cup oats	240 ml
1¼ cups crushed corn flakes	300 ml

Instructions for jar:

- Spoon sugar into 1-quart (1 L) jar.
- Layer brown sugar over sugar.
- Combine flour, baking powder, baking soda and salt. Spoon over brown sugar.
- Spoon oats over flour mixture and top with corn flakes.

♥ *Decorate jar using the suggestions and tips found on pages 4 and 5.*

Crisp Coconut Cookies

Instructions for baking:

½ cup (1 stick) butter, melted	**120 ml**
1 egg	
1 teaspoon vanilla	**5 ml**

- Preheat oven to 350° (176°C).

- Empty contents of jar into mixing bowl and stir to combine.

- Beat butter, egg and vanilla in large mixing bowl.

- Slowly add dry ingredients to egg mixture and mix well after each addition.

- Drop dough by teaspoonfuls on sprayed baking sheet and bake for 10 minutes or until cookies are light brown.

"The most beautiful thing we can experience is the mysterious, it is the true source of art, science, and friendship."
- Albert Einstien

Crisp Coconut Cookies

Instructions for baking:

½ cup (1 stick) butter, melted	120 ml
1 egg	
1 teaspoon vanilla	5 ml

- Preheat oven to 350° (176°C).
- Empty contents of jar into mixing bowl and stir to combine.
- Beat butter, egg and vanilla in large mixing bowl.
- Slowly add dry ingredients to egg mixture and mix well after each addition
- Drop dough by teaspoonfuls on sprayed baking sheet and bake for 10 minutes or until cookies are light brown.

- ✂

Crisp Coconut Cookies

Instructions for baking:

½ cup (1 stick) butter, melted	120 ml
1 egg	
1 teaspoon vanilla	5 ml

- Preheat oven to 350° (176°C).
- Empty contents of jar into mixing bowl and stir to combine.
- Beat butter, egg and vanilla in large mixing bowl.
- Slowly add dry ingredients to egg mixture and mix well after each addition
- Drop dough by teaspoonfuls on sprayed baking sheet and bake for 10 minutes or until cookies are light brown.

- ✂

Crisp Coconut Cookies

Instructions for baking:

½ cup (1 stick) butter, melted	120 ml
1 egg	
1 teaspoon vanilla	5 ml

- Preheat oven to 350° (176°C).
- Empty contents of jar into mixing bowl and stir to combine.
- Beat butter, egg and vanilla in large mixing bowl.
- Slowly add dry ingredients to egg mixture and mix well after each addition
- Drop dough by teaspoonfuls on sprayed baking sheet and bake for 10 minutes or until cookies are light brown.

Crisp Coconut Cookies

Instructions for baking:

½ cup (1 stick) butter, melted	**120 ml**
1 egg	
1 teaspoon vanilla	**5 ml**

- Preheat oven to 350° (176°C).
- Empty contents of jar into mixing bowl and stir to combine.
- Beat butter, egg and vanilla in large mixing bowl.
- Slowly add dry ingredients to egg mixture and mix well after each addition
- Drop dough by teaspoonfuls on sprayed baking sheet and bake for 10 minutes or until cookies are light brown.

www.cookbookresources.com

Crisp Coconut Cookies

Instructions for baking:

½ cup (1 stick) butter, melted	**120 ml**
1 egg	
1 teaspoon vanilla	**5 ml**

- Preheat oven to 350° (176°C).
- Empty contents of jar into mixing bowl and stir to combine.
- Beat butter, egg and vanilla in large mixing bowl.
- Slowly add dry ingredients to egg mixture and mix well after each addition
- Drop dough by teaspoonfuls on sprayed baking sheet and bake for 10 minutes or until cookies are light brown.

www.cookbookresources.com

Crisp Coconut Cookies

Instructions for baking:

½ cup (1 stick) butter, melted	**120 ml**
1 egg	
1 teaspoon vanilla	**5 ml**

- Preheat oven to 350° (176°C).
- Empty contents of jar into mixing bowl and stir to combine.
- Beat butter, egg and vanilla in large mixing bowl.
- Slowly add dry ingredients to egg mixture and mix well after each addition
- Drop dough by teaspoonfuls on sprayed baking sheet and bake for 10 minutes or until cookies are light brown.

www.cookbookresources.com

Peanut Butter Cookies

Peanut Butter Cookies

Here's a classic for the peanut butter lover. These crispy, golden brown treats are an all-time favorite.

Ingredients for jar:

2¼ cups flour	540 ml
1 teaspoon baking soda	5 ml
1 cup packed brown sugar	240 ml
1 cup sugar	240 ml

Instructions for jar:

- Combine flour, baking soda and place in 1-quart (1 L) jar.

- Spoon brown sugar over flour mixture.

- Spoon sugar over brown sugar.

♥ *Decorate jar using the suggestions and tips found on pages 4 and 5.*

Peanut Butter Cookies

Instructions for baking:

1 cup (2 sticks) butter, softened	**240 ml**
1 cup crunchy or smooth peanut butter	**240 ml**
2 eggs	

- Preheat oven to 350° (176°C).

- Empty contents of jar into large mixing bowl.

- In small bowl, blend butter, peanut butter and eggs. (To blend easier, warm butter and peanut butter in microwave for 40 seconds before you mix with eggs.)

- Stir butter mixture into dry ingredients and mix well.

- Roll teaspoonfuls of dough into balls. Place on sprayed baking sheet. Make crisscross shape on each by flattening with fork dipped in sugar.

- Bake for 12 to 13 minutes.

"What helps us in friendship is not so much the help our friends give but the confident knowledge that they will help us."

- Epicurus

Peanut Butter Cookies

Instructions for baking:

1 cup (2 sticks) butter, softened	**240 ml**
1 cup crunchy or smooth peanut butter	**240 ml**
2 eggs	

- Preheat oven to 350°(176°C).
- Empty contents of jar into large mixing bowl.
- In small bowl, blend butter, peanut butter and eggs. (To blend easier, warm butter and peanut butter in microwave for 40 seconds before you mix with eggs.)
- Stir butter mixture into dry ingredients and mix well.
- Roll teaspoonfuls of dough into balls. Place on sprayed baking sheet. Make crisscross shape on each by flattening with fork dipped in sugar.
- Bake for 12 to 13 minutes.

www.cookbookresources.com

- ✂

Peanut Butter Cookies

Instructions for baking:

1 cup (2 sticks) butter, softened	**240 ml**
1 cup crunchy or smooth peanut butter	**240 ml**
2 eggs	

- Preheat oven to 350°(176°C).
- Empty contents of jar into large mixing bowl.
- In small bowl, blend butter, peanut butter and eggs. (To blend easier, warm butter and peanut butter in microwave for 40 seconds before you mix with eggs.)
- Stir butter mixture into dry ingredients and mix well.
- Roll teaspoonfuls of dough into balls. Place on sprayed baking sheet. Make crisscross shape on each by flattening with fork dipped in sugar.
- Bake for 12 to 13 minutes.

www.cookbookresources.com

- ✂

Peanut Butter Cookies

Instructions for baking:

1 cup (2 sticks) butter, softened	**240 ml**
1 cup crunchy or smooth peanut butter	**240 ml**
2 eggs	

- Preheat oven to 350°(176°C).
- Empty contents of jar into large mixing bowl.
- In small bowl, blend butter, peanut butter and eggs. (To blend easier, warm butter and peanut butter in microwave for 40 seconds before you mix with eggs.)
- Stir butter mixture into dry ingredients and mix well.
- Roll teaspoonfuls of dough into balls. Place on sprayed baking sheet. Make crisscross shape on each by flattening with fork dipped in sugar.
- Bake for 12 to 13 minutes.

www.cookbookresources.com

Peanut Butter Cookies

Instructions for baking:

1 cup (2 sticks) butter, softened   240 ml
1 cup crunchy or smooth peanut butter   240 ml
2 eggs

- Preheat oven to 350°(176°C).
- Empty contents of jar into large mixing bowl.
- In small bowl, blend butter, peanut butter and eggs. (To blend easier, warm butter and peanut butter in microwave for 40 seconds before you mix with eggs.)
- Stir butter mixture into dry ingredients and mix well.
- Roll teaspoonfuls of dough into balls. Place on sprayed baking sheet. Make crisscross shape on each by flattening with fork dipped in sugar.
- Bake for 12 to 13 minutes.

www.cookbookresources.com

Peanut Butter Cookies

Instructions for baking:

1 cup (2 sticks) butter, softened   240 ml
1 cup crunchy or smooth peanut butter   240 ml
2 eggs

- Preheat oven to 350°(176°C).
- Empty contents of jar into large mixing bowl.
- In small bowl, blend butter, peanut butter and eggs. (To blend easier, warm butter and peanut butter in microwave for 40 seconds before you mix with eggs.)
- Stir butter mixture into dry ingredients and mix well.
- Roll teaspoonfuls of dough into balls. Place on sprayed baking sheet. Make crisscross shape on each by flattening with fork dipped in sugar.
- Bake for 12 to 13 minutes.

www.cookbookresources.com

Peanut Butter Cookies

Instructions for baking:

1 cup (2 sticks) butter, softened   240 ml
1 cup crunchy or smooth peanut butter   240 ml
2 eggs

- Preheat oven to 350°(176°C).
- Empty contents of jar into large mixing bowl.
- In small bowl, blend butter, peanut butter and eggs. (To blend easier, warm butter and peanut butter in microwave for 40 seconds before you mix with eggs.)
- Stir butter mixture into dry ingredients and mix well.
- Roll teaspoonfuls of dough into balls. Place on sprayed baking sheet. Make crisscross shape on each by flattening with fork dipped in sugar.
- Bake for 12 to 13 minutes.

www.cookbookresources.com

Tangy Lemonade Cookies

Tangy Lemonade Cookies

Ingredients for jar:

1 cup sugar	240 ml
¼ cup chopped pecans	60 ml
3 cups flour	710 ml
1 teaspoon baking soda	5 ml
¼ teaspoon salt	1 ml

Instructions for jar:

- Spoon sugar into 1-quart (1 L) jar.

- Sprinkle pecans over sugar.

- Mix flour with baking soda and salt and spoon over sugar.

♥ *Decorate jar using the suggestions and tips found on pages 4 and 5.*

Tangy Lemonade Cookies

Instructions for baking:

1 cup (2 sticks) butter, softened	240 ml
2 eggs, beaten	
1 (6 ounce) can frozen lemonade, concentrate, thawed, divided	168 g
½ cup sugar	120 ml

- Preheat oven to 350° (176°C).

- Empty contents of jar into large bowl and stir to mix.

- Add eggs and ½ cup (120 ml) lemonade concentrate to dry ingredients. Stir well.

- Drop dough by teaspoonfuls onto ungreased baking sheet and bake for 8 minutes or until cookies are light brown around edges.

- Remove from oven, brush hot cookies lightly with remaining lemonade concentrate and sprinkle with sugar.

- Move to cooling rack.

"Try not to become a man of success but rather try to become a man of value."
- Albert Einstein

Tangy Lemonade Cookies

Instructions for baking:

1 cup (2 sticks) butter, softened	240 ml
2 eggs, beaten	
1 (6 ounce) can frozen lemonade concentrate, thawed, divided	168 g
½ cup sugar	120 ml

- Preheat oven to 350° (176°C).
- Empty contents of jar into large bowl and stir to mix.
- Add eggs and ½ cup (120 ml) lemonade concentrate to dry ingredients. Stir well.
- Drop dough by teaspoonfuls onto ungreased baking sheet and bake for 8 minutes, or until cookies are light brown around edges.
- Remove from oven, brush hot cookies lightly with remaining lemonade concentrate and sprinkle with sugar.
- Move to cooling rack.   www.cookbookresources.com

Tangy Lemonade Cookies

Instructions for baking:

1 cup (2 sticks) butter, softened	240 ml
2 eggs, beaten	
1 (6 ounce) can frozen lemonade concentrate, thawed, divided	168 g
½ cup sugar	120 ml

- Preheat oven to 350° (176°C).
- Empty contents of jar into large bowl and stir to mix.
- Add eggs and ½ cup (120 ml) lemonade concentrate to dry ingredients. Stir well.
- Drop dough by teaspoonfuls onto ungreased baking sheet and bake for 8 minutes, or until cookies are light brown around edges.
- Remove from oven, brush hot cookies lightly with remaining lemonade concentrate and sprinkle with sugar.
- Move to cooling rack.   www.cookbookresources.com

Tangy Lemonade Cookies

Instructions for baking:

1 cup (2 sticks) butter, softened	240 ml
2 eggs, beaten	
1 (6 ounce) can frozen lemonade concentrate, thawed, divided	168 g
½ cup sugar	120 ml

- Preheat oven to 350° (176°C).
- Empty contents of jar into large bowl and stir to mix.
- Add eggs and ½ cup (120 ml) lemonade concentrate to dry ingredients. Stir well.
- Drop dough by teaspoonfuls onto ungreased baking sheet and bake for 8 minutes, or until cookies are light brown around edges.
- Remove from oven, brush hot cookies lightly with remaining lemonade concentrate and sprinkle with sugar.
- Move to cooling rack.   www.cookbookresources.com

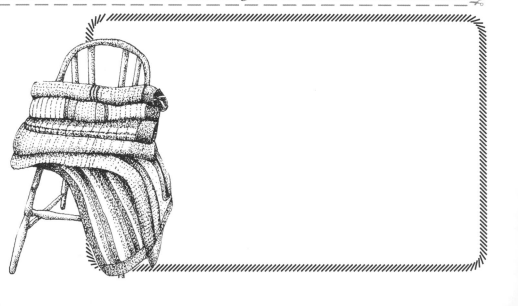

Tangy Lemonade Cookies

Instructions for baking:

1 cup (2 sticks) butter, softened	240 ml
2 eggs, beaten	
1 (6 ounce) can frozen lemonade concentrate, thawed, divided	168 g
½ cup sugar	120 ml

- Preheat oven to 350° (176°C).
- Empty contents of jar into large bowl and stir to mix.
- Add eggs and ½ cup (120 ml) lemonade concentrate to dry ingredients. Stir well.
- Drop dough by teaspoonfuls onto ungreased baking sheet and bake for 8 minutes, or until cookies are light brown around edges.
- Remove from oven, brush hot cookies lightly with remaining lemonade concentrate and sprinkle with sugar.
- Move to cooling rack.

www.cookbookresources.com

Tangy Lemonade Cookies

Instructions for baking:

1 cup (2 sticks) butter, softened	240 ml
2 eggs, beaten	
1 (6 ounce) can frozen lemonade concentrate, thawed, divided	168 g
½ cup sugar	120 ml

- Preheat oven to 350° (176°C).
- Empty contents of jar into large bowl and stir to mix.
- Add eggs and ½ cup (120 ml) lemonade concentrate to dry ingredients. Stir well.
- Drop dough by teaspoonfuls onto ungreased baking sheet and bake for 8 minutes, or until cookies are light brown around edges.
- Remove from oven, brush hot cookies lightly with remaining lemonade concentrate and sprinkle with sugar.
- Move to cooling rack.

www.cookbookresources.com

Tangy Lemonade Cookies

Instructions for baking:

1 cup (2 sticks) butter, softened	240 ml
2 eggs, beaten	
1 (6 ounce) can frozen lemonade concentrate, thawed, divided	168 g
½ cup sugar	120 ml

- Preheat oven to 350° (176°C).
- Empty contents of jar into large bowl and stir to mix.
- Add eggs and ½ cup (120 ml) lemonade concentrate to dry ingredients. Stir well.
- Drop dough by teaspoonfuls onto ungreased baking sheet and bake for 8 minutes, or until cookies are light brown around edges.
- Remove from oven, brush hot cookies lightly with remaining lemonade concentrate and sprinkle with sugar.
- Move to cooling rack.

www.cookbookresources.com

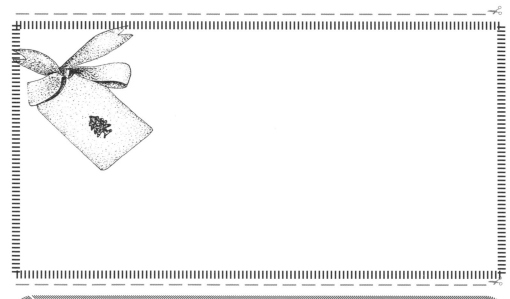

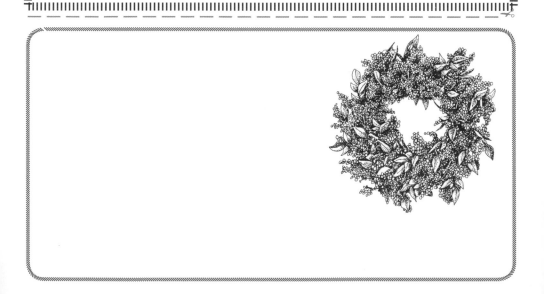

No-Bake Chocolate Cookies

No-Bake Chocolate Cookies

Ingredients for jar:

3 cups quick-cooking oats	710 ml
¼ cup cocoa powder	60 ml
1 cup shredded, sweetened coconut	240 ml
½ teaspoon salt	2 ml

Instructions for jar:

- Spoon oats into 1-quart jar.

- Layer cocoa powder over oats.

- Spoon coconut over cocoa powder.

- Add salt.

♥ *Decorate jar using the suggestions and tips found on pages 4 and 5.*

No-Bake Chocolate Cookies

Instructions for making cookies:

2 cups sugar	**480 ml**
½ cup milk	**120 ml**
½ cup (1 stick) butter	**120 ml**

- Combine sugar, milk and butter in saucepan and bring to a boil. Stir frequently. Boil over medium heat for 3 minutes.

- Remove from heat.

- Add ingredients from jar and mix well.

- Working quickly, drop by heaping tablespoonfuls onto wax paper or sprayed baking sheet.

" Help thy brothers boat across, and lo, thine own has reached the shore."
  - Old Hindu proverb

No-Bake Chocolate Cookies

Instructions for making cookies:

2 cups sugar	**480 ml**
½ cup milk	**120 ml**
½ cup (1 stick) butter	**120 ml**

- Combine sugar, milk and butter in saucepan and bring to a boil. Stir frequently. Boil over medium heat for 3 minutes.
- Remove from heat.
- Add ingredients from jar and mix well.
- Working quickly, drop by heaping tablespoonfuls onto wax paper or sprayed baking sheet.

www.cookbookresources.com

No-Bake Chocolate Cookies

Instructions for making cookies:

2 cups sugar	**480 ml**
½ cup milk	**120 ml**
½ cup (1 stick) butter	**120 ml**

- Combine sugar, milk and butter in saucepan and bring to a boil. Stir frequently. Boil over medium heat for 3 minutes.
- Remove from heat.
- Add ingredients from jar and mix well.
- Working quickly, drop by heaping tablespoonfuls onto wax paper or sprayed baking sheet.

www.cookbookresources.com

No-Bake Chocolate Cookies

Instructions for making cookies:

2 cups sugar	**480 ml**
½ cup milk	**120 ml**
½ cup (1 stick) butter	**120 ml**

- Combine sugar, milk and butter in saucepan and bring to a boil. Stir frequently. Boil over medium heat for 3 minutes.
- Remove from heat.
- Add ingredients from jar and mix well.
- Working quickly, drop by heaping tablespoonfuls onto wax paper or sprayed baking sheet.

www.cookbookresources.com

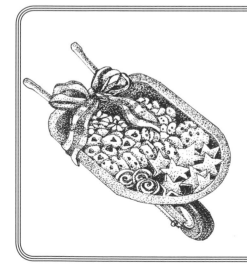

No-Bake Chocolate Cookies

Instructions for making cookies:

2 cups sugar	**480 ml**
½ cup milk	**120 ml**
½ cup (1 stick) butter	**120 ml**

- Combine sugar, milk and butter in saucepan and bring to a boil. Stir frequently. Boil over medium heat for 3 minutes.
- Remove from heat.
- Add ingredients from jar and mix well.
- Working quickly, drop by heaping tablespoonfuls onto wax paper or sprayed baking sheet.

www.cookbookresources.com

No-Bake Chocolate Cookies

Instructions for making cookies:

2 cups sugar	**480 ml**
½ cup milk	**120 ml**
½ cup (1 stick) butter	**120 ml**

- Combine sugar, milk and butter in saucepan and bring to a boil. Stir frequently. Boil over medium heat for 3 minutes.
- Remove from heat.
- Add ingredients from jar and mix well.
- Working quickly, drop by heaping tablespoonfuls onto wax paper or sprayed baking sheet.

www.cookbookresources.com

No-Bake Chocolate Cookies

Instructions for making cookies:

2 cups sugar	**480 ml**
½ cup milk	**120 ml**
½ cup (1 stick) butter	**120 ml**

- Combine sugar, milk and butter in saucepan and bring to a boil. Stir frequently. Boil over medium heat for 3 minutes.
- Remove from heat.
- Add ingredients from jar and mix well.
- Working quickly, drop by heaping tablespoonfuls onto wax paper or sprayed baking sheet.

www.cookbookresources.com

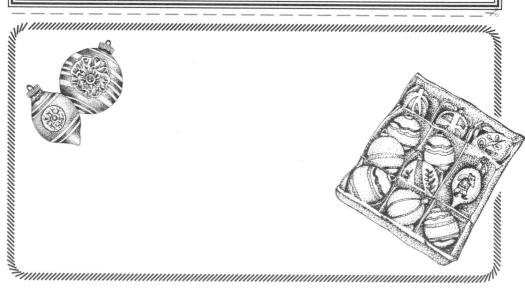

Old-Fashioned Tea Cakes

Old-Fashioned Tea Cakes

Ingredients for jar:

3¼ cups flour	770 ml
1 teaspoon baking soda	5 ml
½ teaspoon salt	2 ml
1 cup sugar	240 ml

Instructions for jar:

- Sift flour, baking soda, salt and sugar.

- Spoon mixture into 1-quart (1 L) jar.

♥ *Decorate jar using the suggestions and tips found on pages 4 and 5.*

Old-Fashioned Tea Cakes

Instructions for baking:

½ **cup (1 stick) butter, softened**	**120 ml**
1 egg, beaten	
1½ teaspoons vanilla	**7 ml**
½ **cup sour cream**	**120 ml**

■ Preheat oven to 350° (176°C).

■ In large bowl, combine butter, egg and vanilla. Beat on medium speed for 2 minutes.

■ Stir in sour cream.

■ Slowly add dry ingredients from jar into sour cream mixture and stir well after each addition.

■ On lightly floured surface, roll dough to ¼-inch (.6 cm) thickness.

■ Cut cookies with floured cookie cutter and place on sprayed baking sheet.

■ Bake for 10 to 12 minutes. Remove from oven before cookies become too brown.

"There is nothing like a dream to create the future."
- Victor Hugo

Old-Fashioned Tea Cakes

Instructions for baking:

½ cup (1 stick) butter, softened	120 ml
1 egg, beaten	
1½ teaspoons vanilla	7 ml
½ cup sour cream	120 ml

- Preheat oven to 350° (176°C).
- In large bowl, combine butter, egg and vanilla. Beat on medium speed for 2 minutes.
- Stir in sour cream.
- Slowly add dry ingredients from jar into sour cream mixture and stir well after each addition.
- On lightly floured surface, roll dough to ¼-inch (.6 cm) thickness.
- Cut cookies with floured cookie cutter and place on sprayed baking sheet.
- Bake for 10 to 12 minutes. Remove from oven before cookies become too brown.

www.cookbookresources.com

Old-Fashioned Tea Cakes

Instructions for baking:

½ cup (1 stick) butter, softened	120 ml
1 egg, beaten	
1½ teaspoons vanilla	7 ml
½ cup sour cream	120 ml

- Preheat oven to 350° (176°C).
- In large bowl, combine butter, egg and vanilla. Beat on medium speed for 2 minutes.
- Stir in sour cream.
- Slowly add dry ingredients from jar into sour cream mixture and stir well after each addition.
- On lightly floured surface, roll dough to ¼-inch (.6 cm) thickness.
- Cut cookies with floured cookie cutter and place on sprayed baking sheet.
- Bake for 10 to 12 minutes. Remove from oven before cookies become too brown.

www.cookbookresources.com

Old-Fashioned Tea Cakes

Instructions for baking:

½ cup (1 stick) butter, softened	120 ml
1 egg, beaten	
1½ teaspoons vanilla	7 ml
½ cup sour cream	120 ml

- Preheat oven to 350° (176°C).
- In large bowl, combine butter, egg and vanilla. Beat on medium speed for 2 minutes.
- Stir in sour cream.
- Slowly add dry ingredients from jar into sour cream mixture and stir well after each addition.
- On lightly floured surface, roll dough to ¼-inch (.6 cm) thickness.
- Cut cookies with floured cookie cutter and place on sprayed baking sheet.
- Bake for 10 to 12 minutes. Remove from oven before cookies become too brown.

www.cookbookresources.com

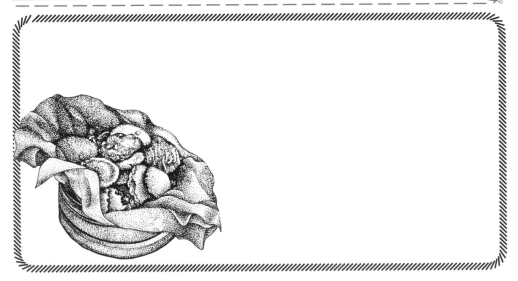

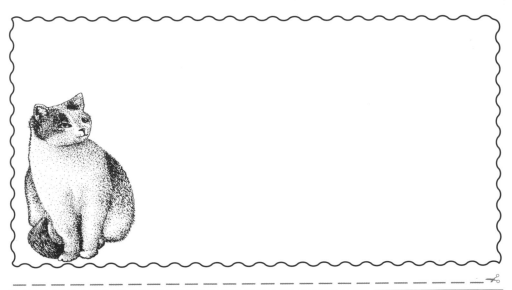

Old-Fashioned Tea Cakes

Instructions for baking:

½ cup (1 stick) butter, softened	120 ml
1 egg, beaten	
1½ teaspoons vanilla	7 ml
½ cup sour cream	120 ml

- Preheat oven to 350° (176°C).
- In large bowl, combine butter, egg and vanilla. Beat on medium speed for 2 minutes.
- Stir in sour cream.
- Slowly add dry ingredients from jar into sour cream mixture and stir well after each addition.
- On lightly floured surface, roll dough to ¼-inch (.6 cm) thickness.
- Cut cookies with floured cookie cutter and place on sprayed baking sheet.
- Bake for 10 to 12 minutes. Remove from oven before cookies become too brown.

www.cookbookresources.com

Old-Fashioned Tea Cakes

Instructions for baking:

½ cup (1 stick) butter, softened	120 ml
1 egg, beaten	
1½ teaspoons vanilla	7 ml
½ cup sour cream	120 ml

- Preheat oven to 350° (176°C).
- In large bowl, combine butter, egg and vanilla. Beat on medium speed for 2 minutes.
- Stir in sour cream.
- Slowly add dry ingredients from jar into sour cream mixture and stir well after each addition.
- On lightly floured surface, roll dough to ¼-inch (.6 cm) thickness.
- Cut cookies with floured cookie cutter and place on sprayed baking sheet.
- Bake for 10 to 12 minutes. Remove from oven before cookies become too brown.

www.cookbookresources.com

Old-Fashioned Tea Cakes

Instructions for baking:

½ cup (1 stick) butter, softened	120 ml
1 egg, beaten	
1½ teaspoons vanilla	7 ml
½ cup sour cream	120 ml

- Preheat oven to 350° (176°C).
- In large bowl, combine butter, egg and vanilla. Beat on medium speed for 2 minutes.
- Stir in sour cream.
- Slowly add dry ingredients from jar into sour cream mixture and stir well after each addition.
- On lightly floured surface, roll dough to ¼-inch (.6 cm) thickness.
- Cut cookies with floured cookie cutter and place on sprayed baking sheet.
- Bake for 10 to 12 minutes. Remove from oven before cookies become too brown.

www.cookbookresources.com

Oatmeal-Raisin Crisps

Oatmeal-Raisin Crisps

Ingredients for jar:

1 cup flour	240 ml
1 teaspoon baking soda	5 ml
½ teaspoon salt	2 ml
1 cup quick-cooking oats	240 ml
1 cup crisped rice cereal	240 ml
½ cup packed brown sugar	120 ml
½ cup sugar	120 ml
¼ cup raisins	60 ml

Instructions for jar:

■ Combine flour, baking soda and salt. Spoon into 1-quart (1 L) jar.

■ Layer following ingredients over flour mixture: oats, cereal, brown sugar, sugar and raisins. (Press down gently to fit.)

♥ *Decorate jar using the suggestions and tips found on pages 4 and 5.*

Oatmeal-Raisin Crisps

Instructions for baking:

½ cup (1 stick) butter, softened	**120 ml**
1 egg	
1 teaspoon vanilla	**5 ml**

- Preheat oven to 350° (176°C).

- Empty contents of jar into large bowl.

- Beat egg with butter and vanilla.

- Stir egg mixture into dry ingredients and mix well.

- Roll teaspoonfuls of dough into 1-inch (2.5 cm) balls and place on sprayed baking sheet.

- Bake for 10 to 15 minutes or until cookies are golden brown.

"For he who looks into the face of a friend, beholds, as it were, a copy of himself."

- Cicero

Oatmeal-Raisin Crisps

Instructions for baking:

½ cup (1 stick) butter, softened	120 ml
1 egg	
1 teaspoon vanilla	5 ml

- Preheat oven to 350° (176°C).
- Empty contents of jar into large bowl.
- Beat egg with butter and vanilla.
- Stir egg mixture into dry ingredients and mix well.
- Roll teaspoonfuls of dough into 1-inch (2.5 cm) balls and place on sprayed baking sheet.
- Bake for 10 to 15 minutes or until cookies are golden brown.

www.cookbookresources.com

Oatmeal-Raisin Crisps

Instructions for baking:

½ cup (1 stick) butter, softened	120 ml
1 egg	
1 teaspoon vanilla	5 ml

- Preheat oven to 350° (176°C).
- Empty contents of jar into large bowl.
- Beat egg with butter and vanilla.
- Stir egg mixture into dry ingredients and mix well.
- Roll teaspoonfuls of dough into 1-inch (2.5 cm) balls and place on sprayed baking sheet.
- Bake for 10 to 15 minutes or until cookies are golden brown.

www.cookbookresources.com

Oatmeal-Raisin Crisps

Instructions for baking:

½ cup (1 stick) butter, softened	120 ml
1 egg	
1 teaspoon vanilla	5 ml

- Preheat oven to 350° (176°C).
- Empty contents of jar into large bowl.
- Beat egg with butter and vanilla.
- Stir egg mixture into dry ingredients and mix well.
- Roll teaspoonfuls of dough into 1-inch (2.5 cm) balls and place on sprayed baking sheet.
- Bake for 10 to 15 minutes or until cookies are golden brown.

www.cookbookresources.com

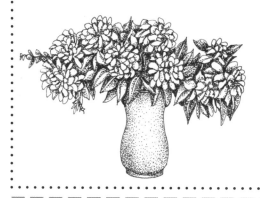

Oatmeal-Raisin Crisps

Instructions for baking:

½ cup (1 stick) butter, softened	120 ml
1 egg	
1 teaspoon vanilla	5 ml

- Preheat oven to 350° (176°C).
- Empty contents of jar into large bowl.
- Beat egg with butter and vanilla.
- Stir egg mixture into dry ingredients and mix well.
- Roll teaspoonfuls of dough into 1-inch (2.5 cm) balls and place on sprayed baking sheet.
- Bake for 10 to 15 minutes or until cookies are golden brown.

- ✂

Oatmeal-Raisin Crisps

Instructions for baking:

½ cup (1 stick) butter, softened	120 ml
1 egg	
1 teaspoon vanilla	5 ml

- Preheat oven to 350° (176°C).
- Empty contents of jar into large bowl.
- Beat egg with butter and vanilla.
- Stir egg mixture into dry ingredients and mix well.
- Roll teaspoonfuls of dough into 1-inch (2.5 cm) balls and place on sprayed baking sheet.
- Bake for 10 to 15 minutes or until cookies are golden brown.

www.cookbookresources.com

- ✂

Oatmeal-Raisin Crisps

Instructions for baking:

½ cup (1 stick) butter, softened	120 ml
1 egg	
1 teaspoon vanilla	5 ml

- Preheat oven to 350° (176°C).
- Empty contents of jar into large bowl.
- Beat egg with butter and vanilla.
- Stir egg mixture into dry ingredients and mix well.
- Roll teaspoonfuls of dough into 1-inch (2.5 cm) balls and place on sprayed baking sheet.
- Bake for 10 to 15 minutes or until cookies are golden brown.

www.cookbookresources.com

Crackled Brownie Bites

Crackled Brownie Bites

These little chocolate mounds are moist and brownie-like in texture. They also have an interesting crackle look on the outside.

Ingredients for jar:

1 cup sugar	240 ml
¾ cup cocoa powder	180 ml
1 cup flour	240 ml
1 teaspoon baking powder	5 ml
½ teaspoon salt	2 ml
1 cup chopped pecans	240 ml
½ cup miniature chocolate chips	120 ml

Instructions for jar:

- Place sugar in 1-quart (1 L) jar.

- Spoon cocoa powder over sugar.

- Combine flour, baking powder and salt and then spoon over cocoa powder.

- Layer chocolate chips over flour.

Crackled Brownie Bites

Instructions for baking:

6 tablespoons (¾ stick) butter, melted	**90 ml**
2 eggs	
1 teaspoon vanilla	**5 ml**
½ cup sifted powdered sugar	**120 ml**

- Empty contents of jar into large mixing bowl. Stir to combine ingredients.

- In small bowl, mix butter, eggs and vanilla.

- Add butter mixture to dry ingredients and stir well. Dough will be very stiff.

- Cover and chill dough for 2 to 3 hours.

- To bake, preheat oven to 350° (176°C).

- Take teaspoonfuls of dough and shape into balls. Roll balls in powdered sugar and place on sprayed baking sheet.

- Bake for 12 to 13 minutes. Remove from oven and cool on baking sheet for 1 minute before moving to cooling rack.

"A smile is an inexpensive way to improve your looks."

- Anonymous

Crackled Brownie Bites

Instructions for baking:

6 tablespoons (¾ stick) butter, melted	90 ml
2 eggs	
1 teaspoon vanilla	5 ml
½ cup sifted powdered sugar	120 ml

- Empty contents of jar into large mixing bowl. Stir to combine ingredients.
- In small bowl, mix butter, eggs and vanilla.
- Add butter mixture to dry ingredients and stir well. Dough will be very stiff.
- Cover and chill dough for 2 to 3 hours.
- To bake, preheat oven to 350° (176°C).
- Take teaspoonfuls of dough and shape into balls. Roll balls in powdered sugar and place on sprayed baking sheet.
- Bake for 12 to 13 minutes. Remove from oven and cool on baking sheet for 1 minute before moving to cooling rack.

www.cookbookresources.com

- -

Crackled Brownie Bites

Instructions for baking:

6 tablespoons (¾ stick) butter, melted	90 ml
2 eggs	
1 teaspoon vanilla	5 ml
½ cup sifted powdered sugar	120 ml

- Empty contents of jar into large mixing bowl. Stir to combine ingredients.
- In small bowl, mix butter, eggs and vanilla.
- Add butter mixture to dry ingredients and stir well. Dough will be very stiff.
- Cover and chill dough for 2 to 3 hours.
- To bake, preheat oven to 350° (176°C).
- Take teaspoonfuls of dough and shape into balls. Roll balls in powdered sugar and place on sprayed baking sheet.
- Bake for 12 to 13 minutes. Remove from oven and cool on baking sheet for 1 minute before moving to cooling rack.

www.cookbookresources.com

- -

Crackled Brownie Bites

Instructions for baking:

6 tablespoons (¾ stick) butter, melted	90 ml
2 eggs	
1 teaspoon vanilla	5 ml
½ cup sifted powdered sugar	120 ml

- Empty contents of jar into large mixing bowl. Stir to combine ingredients.
- In small bowl, mix butter, eggs and vanilla.
- Add butter mixture to dry ingredients and stir well. Dough will be very stiff.
- Cover and chill dough for 2 to 3 hours.
- To bake, preheat oven to 350° (176°C).
- Take teaspoonfuls of dough and shape into balls. Roll balls in powdered sugar and place on sprayed baking sheet.
- Bake for 12 to 13 minutes. Remove from oven and cool on baking sheet for 1 minute before moving to cooling rack.

www.cookbookresources.com

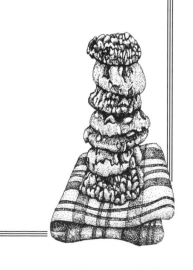

Crackled Brownie Bites

Instructions for baking:

6 tablespoons (¾ stick) butter, melted	90 ml
2 eggs	
1 teaspoon vanilla	5 ml
½ cup sifted powdered sugar	120 ml

- Empty contents of jar into large mixing bowl. Stir to combine ingredients.
- In small bowl, mix butter, eggs and vanilla.
- Add butter mixture to dry ingredients and stir well. Dough will be very stiff.
- Cover and chill dough for 2 to 3 hours.
- To bake, preheat oven to 350° (176°C).
- Take teaspoonfuls of dough and shape into balls. Roll balls in powdered sugar and place on sprayed baking sheet.
- Bake for 12 to 13 minutes. Remove from oven and cool on baking sheet for 1 minute before moving to cooling rack.

www.cookbookresources.com

- ✂

Crackled Brownie Bites

Instructions for baking:

6 tablespoons (¾ stick) butter, melted	90 ml
2 eggs	
1 teaspoon vanilla	5 ml
½ cup sifted powdered sugar	120 ml

- Empty contents of jar into large mixing bowl. Stir to combine ingredients.
- In small bowl, mix butter, eggs and vanilla.
- Add butter mixture to dry ingredients and stir well. Dough will be very stiff.
- Cover and chill dough for 2 to 3 hours.
- To bake, preheat oven to 350° (176°C).
- Take teaspoonfuls of dough and shape into balls. Roll balls in powdered sugar and place on sprayed baking sheet.
- Bake for 12 to 13 minutes. Remove from oven and cool on baking sheet for 1 minute before moving to cooling rack.

www.cookbookresources.com

- ✂

Crackled Brownie Bites

Instructions for baking:

6 tablespoons (¾ stick) butter, melted	90 ml
2 eggs	
1 teaspoon vanilla	5 ml
½ cup sifted powdered sugar	120 ml

- Empty contents of jar into large mixing bowl. Stir to combine ingredients.
- In small bowl, mix butter, eggs and vanilla.
- Add butter mixture to dry ingredients and stir well. Dough will be very stiff.
- Cover and chill dough for 2 to 3 hours.
- To bake, preheat oven to 350° (176°C).
- Take teaspoonfuls of dough and shape into balls. Roll balls in powdered sugar and place on sprayed baking sheet.
- Bake for 12 to 13 minutes. Remove from oven and cool on baking sheet for 1 minute before moving to cooling rack.

www.cookbookresources.com

Nutty Buttery Bites

Nutty Buttery Bites

These ball cookies are delicate both in form and flavor.

Ingredients for jar:

²/₃ cup sugar	160 ml
1½ cups finely chopped pecans	360 ml
2 cups flour	480 ml
¼ teaspoon salt	1 ml

Instructions for jar:

- Spoon sugar into 1-quart (1 L) jar.

- Sprinkle pecans over sugar.

- Combine flour with salt, spoon over pecans and press gently to fil.

♥ *Decorate jar using the suggestions and tips found on pages 4 and 5.*

Nutty Buttery Bites

Instructions for baking:

1 cup (2 sticks) butter, softened	240 ml
1 teaspoon almond extract	5 ml
1 teaspoon vanilla	5 ml
½ to ¾ cup powdered sugar	120-180 ml

- Preheat oven to 350° (176°C).

- Empty contents of jar into large mixing bowl.

- Add butter, almond extract and vanilla to dry ingredients in bowl and mix well. Dough will be slightly crumbly. Knead it a little to make it hold its shape.

- Chill for 1 to 2 hours to make dough easier to handle.

- Take small pieces of dough and shape into 1-inch (2.5 cm) balls.

- Place dough balls on ungreased baking sheet.

- Bake for 12 to 14 minutes or until cookies are light brown.

- While cookies are warm, roll in powdered sugar.

" Side by side or miles apart, dear friends are always close in heart."

- Anonymous

Nutty Buttery Bites

Instructions for baking:

1 cup (2 sticks) butter, softened	240 ml
1 teaspoon almond extract	5 ml
1 teaspoon vanilla	5 ml
½ to ¾ cup powdered sugar	120-180 ml

- Preheat oven to 350°(176°C).
- Empty contents of jar into large mixing bowl.
- Add butter, almond extract and vanilla to dry ingredients in bowl and mix well. Dough will be slightly crumbly. Knead it a little to make it hold its shape.
- Chill for 1 to 2 hours to make dough easier to handle.
- Take small pieces of dough and shape into 1-inch (2.5 cm) balls.
- Place dough balls on ungreased baking sheet.
- Bake for 12 to 14 minutes or until cookies are light brown.
- While cookies are warm, roll in powdered sugar.

www.cookbookresources.com

- ✂

Nutty Buttery Bites

Instructions for baking:

1 cup (2 sticks) butter, softened	240 ml
1 teaspoon almond extract	5 ml
1 teaspoon vanilla	5 ml
½ to ¾ cup powdered sugar	120-180 ml

- Preheat oven to 350°(176°C).
- Empty contents of jar into large mixing bowl.
- Add butter, almond extract and vanilla to dry ingredients in bowl and mix well. Dough will be slightly crumbly. Knead it a little to make it hold its shape.
- Chill for 1 to 2 hours to make dough easier to handle.
- Take small pieces of dough and shape into 1-inch (2.5 cm) balls.
- Place dough balls on ungreased baking sheet.
- Bake for 12 to 14 minutes or until cookies are light brown.
- While cookies are warm, roll in powdered sugar.

www.cookbookresources.com

- ✂

Nutty Buttery Bites

Instructions for baking:

1 cup (2 sticks) butter, softened	240 ml
1 teaspoon almond extract	5 ml
1 teaspoon vanilla	5 ml
½ to ¾ cup powdered sugar	120-180 ml

- Preheat oven to 350°(176°C).
- Empty contents of jar into large mixing bowl.
- Add butter, almond extract and vanilla to dry ingredients in bowl and mix well. Dough will be slightly crumbly. Knead it a little to make it hold its shape.
- Chill for 1 to 2 hours to make dough easier to handle.
- Take small pieces of dough and shape into 1-inch (2.5 cm) balls.
- Place dough balls on ungreased baking sheet.
- Bake for 12 to 14 minutes or until cookies are light brown.
- While cookies are warm, roll in powdered sugar.

www.cookbookresources.com

Nutty Buttery Bites

Instructions for baking:

1 cup (2 sticks) butter, softened	240 ml
1 teaspoon almond extract	5 ml
1 teaspoon vanilla	5 ml
½ to ¾ cup powdered sugar	120-180 ml

- Preheat oven to 350°(176°C).
- Empty contents of jar into large mixing bowl.
- Add butter, almond extract and vanilla to dry ingredients in bowl and mix well. Dough will be slightly crumbly. Knead it a little to make it hold its shape.
- Chill for 1 to 2 hours to make dough easier to handle.
- Take small pieces of dough and shape into 1-inch (2.5 cm) balls.
- Place dough balls on ungreased baking sheet.
- Bake for 12 to 14 minutes or until cookies are light brown.
- While cookies are warm, roll in powdered sugar.

www.cookbookresources.com

Nutty Buttery Bites

Instructions for baking:

1 cup (2 sticks) butter, softened	240 ml
1 teaspoon almond extract	5 ml
1 teaspoon vanilla	5 ml
½ to ¾ cup powdered sugar	120-180 ml

- Preheat oven to 350°(176°C).
- Empty contents of jar into large mixing bowl.
- Add butter, almond extract and vanilla to dry ingredients in bowl and mix well. Dough will be slightly crumbly. Knead it a little to make it hold its shape.
- Chill for 1 to 2 hours to make dough easier to handle.
- Take small pieces of dough and shape into 1-inch (2.5 cm) balls.
- Place dough balls on ungreased baking sheet.
- Bake for 12 to 14 minutes or until cookies are light brown.
- While cookies are warm, roll in powdered sugar.

www.cookbookresources.com

Nutty Buttery Bites

Instructions for baking:

1 cup (2 sticks) butter, softened	240 ml
1 teaspoon almond extract	5 ml
1 teaspoon vanilla	5 ml
½ to ¾ cup powdered sugar	120-180 ml

- Preheat oven to 350°(176°C).
- Empty contents of jar into large mixing bowl.
- Add butter, almond extract and vanilla to dry ingredients in bowl and mix well. Dough will be slightly crumbly. Knead it a little to make it hold its shape.
- Chill for 1 to 2 hours to make dough easier to handle.
- Take small pieces of dough and shape into 1-inch (2.5 cm) balls.
- Place dough balls on ungreased baking sheet.
- Bake for 12 to 14 minutes or until cookies are light brown.
- While cookies are warm, roll in powdered sugar.

www.cookbookresources.com

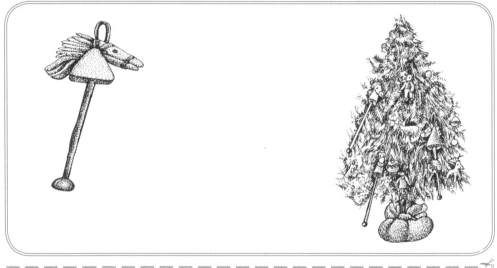

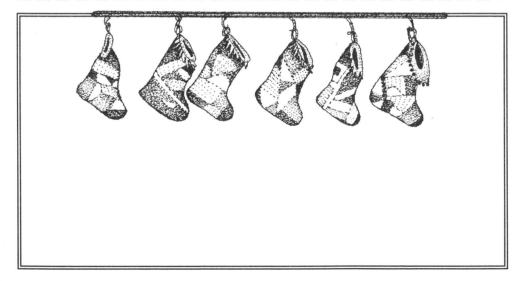

Rum Balls

Rum Balls

*Consider this spirit-filled recipe for the holidays!
For a truly unique gift that's sure to be a hit,
combine the jar of cookie mix in a decorative
holiday basket with a small bottle of rum.*

Ingredients for jar:

3 cups crushed vanilla wafer cookies	710 ml
1¼ cups cocoa powder	300 ml
¾ cup powdered sugar	180 ml
½ cup finely chopped pecans or walnuts	120 ml

Instructions for jar:

■ Put crushed vanilla wafers in 1-quart (1 L) jar.

■ Layer cocoa powder and then powdered sugar over crushed cookies.

■ Top with chopped pecans.

♥ *Decorate jar using the suggestions and tips found on pages 4 and 5.*

Rum Balls

Instructions for making cookies:

3 tablespoons light corn syrup	**45 ml**
½ cup rum (or bourbon)	**120 ml**
Powdered or granulated sugar	

- Empty contents of jar into large mixing bowl. Stir to mix dry ingredients.

- Stir in corn syrup and rum. Blend until dry ingredients are moist.

- Shape dough into 1-inch (2.5 cm) balls and roll in powdered sugar or granulated sugar.

Tip: These look great served in decorative petit fours paper cups. They also taste better as they age. For the best flavor, make them a couple of days before you plan to serve them.

"Do not protect yourself by a fence, but rather by your friends.
- Czech Proverb

Rum Balls

Instructions for making cookies:

3 tablespoons light corn syrup	45 ml
½ cup rum (or bourbon)	120 ml
Powdered or granulated sugar	

- Empty contents of jar into large mixing bowl. Stir to mix dry ingredients.
- Stir in corn syrup and rum. Blend until dry ingredients are moist.
- Shape dough into 1-inch (2.5 cm) balls and roll in powdered sugar or granulated sugar.

Tip: These look great served in decorative petit fours paper cups. They also taste better as they age. For the best flavor, make them a couple of days before you plan to serve them.

www.cookbookresources.com

Rum Balls

Instructions for making cookies:

3 tablespoons light corn syrup	45 ml
½ cup rum (or bourbon)	120 ml
Powdered or granulated sugar	

- Empty contents of jar into large mixing bowl. Stir to mix dry ingredients.
- Stir in corn syrup and rum. Blend until dry ingredients are moist.
- Shape dough into 1-inch (2.5 cm) balls and roll in powdered sugar or granulated sugar.

Tip: These look great served in decorative petit fours paper cups. They also taste better as they age. For the best flavor, make them a couple of days before you plan to serve them.

www.cookbookresources.com

Rum Balls

Instructions for making cookies:

3 tablespoons light corn syrup	45 ml
½ cup rum (or bourbon)	120 ml
Powdered or granulated sugar	

- Empty contents of jar into large mixing bowl. Stir to mix dry ingredients.
- Stir in corn syrup and rum. Blend until dry ingredients are moist.
- Shape dough into 1-inch (2.5 cm) balls and roll in powdered sugar or granulated sugar.

Tip: These look great served in decorative petit fours paper cups. They also taste better as they age. For the best flavor, make them a couple of days before you plan to serve them.

www.cookbookresources.com

Rum Balls

Instructions for making cookies:

3 tablespoons light corn syrup	45 ml
½ cup rum (or bourbon)	120 ml
Powdered or granulated sugar	

- Empty contents of jar into large mixing bowl. Stir to mix dry ingredients.
- Stir in corn syrup and rum. Blend until dry ingredients are moist.
- Shape dough into 1-inch (2.5 cm) balls and roll in powdered sugar or granulated sugar.

Tip: These look great served in decorative petit fours paper cups. They also taste better as they age. For the best flavor, make them a couple of days before you plan to serve them.

www.cookbookresources.com

Rum Balls

Instructions for making cookies:

3 tablespoons light corn syrup	45 ml
½ cup rum (or bourbon)	120 ml
Powdered or granulated sugar	

- Empty contents of jar into large mixing bowl. Stir to mix dry ingredients.
- Stir in corn syrup and rum. Blend until dry ingredients are moist.
- Shape dough into 1-inch (2.5 cm) balls and roll in powdered sugar or granulated sugar.

Tip: These look great served in decorative petit fours paper cups. They also taste better as they age. For the best flavor, make them a couple of days before you plan to serve them.

www.cookbookresources.com

Rum Balls

Instructions for making cookies:

3 tablespoons light corn syrup	45 ml
½ cup rum (or bourbon)	120 ml
Powdered or granulated sugar	

- Empty contents of jar into large mixing bowl. Stir to mix dry ingredients.
- Stir in corn syrup and rum. Blend until dry ingredients are moist.
- Shape dough into 1-inch (2.5 cm) balls and roll in powdered sugar or granulated sugar.

Tip: These look great served in decorative petit fours paper cups. They also taste better as they age. For the best flavor, make them a couple of days before you plan to serve them.

www.cookbookresources.com

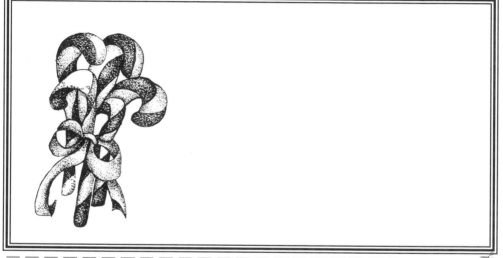

Nutty Crescents

Nutty Crescents

*Don't let the simplicity of this cookie fool
you. It only takes a few ingredients to make a
deliciously light, tasty cookie. This is a great
to make as a gift when time is short.*

Ingredients for jar:

1¼ cups powdered sugar	300 ml
1 cup finely chopped almonds	240 ml
2 cups flour	480 ml

Instructions for jar:

- Combine powdered sugar, almonds and flour.

- Spoon mixture into 1-quart (1 L) jar.

♥ *Decorate jar using the suggestions and tips found
on pages 4 and 5.*

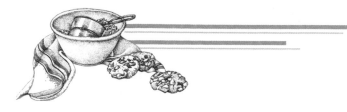

Nutty Crescents

Instructions for baking:

1 cup (2 sticks) butter, softened	**240 ml**
2 teaspoons cold water	**10 ml**
1 teaspoon vanilla	**5 ml**
½ to ¾ cup powdered sugar	**120-180 ml**

- Preheat oven to 350° (176° C).

- Empty contents of jar into large mixing bowl.

- Add butter, water and vanilla to dry ingredients and mix well.

- Dough will be crumbly at first but will hold its shape as you cut butter in.

- Take small pieces of dough and shape into crescents. (To make crescent shapes, roll pieces of dough into 3-inch (8 cm) lengths, place on sprayed baking sheet and shape into half moon, flattening top slightly.

- Bake for 12 to 14 minutes or until cookies are light brown around edges.

- While still warm, coat with powdered sugar. (An easy way to do this is to put cookies in resealable plastic bag with about ½ cup (120 ml) powdered sugar. Seal bag and gently shake to coat.)

Nutty Crescents

Instructions for baking:

1 cup (2 sticks) butter, softened	240 ml
2 teaspoons cold water	10 ml
1 teaspoon vanilla	5 ml
½ to ¾ cup powdered sugar	120-180 ml

- Preheat oven to 350°(176° C).
- Empty contents of jar into large mixing bowl.
- Add butter, water and vanilla to dry ingredients and mix well.
- Dough will be crumbly at first but will hold its shape as you cut butter in.
- Take small pieces of dough and shape into crescents. (To make crescent shapes, roll pieces of dough into 3-inch (8 cm) lengths, place on sprayed baking sheet and shape into half moon, flattening top slightly.
- Bake for 12 to 14 minutes or until cookies are light brown around edges.
- While still warm, coat with powdered sugar. (An easy way to do this is to put cookies in resealable plastic bag with about ½ cup (120 ml) powdered sugar. Seal bag and gently shake to coat.)

www.cookbookresources.com

Nutty Crescents

Instructions for baking:

1 cup (2 sticks) butter, softened	240 ml
2 teaspoons cold water	10 ml
1 teaspoon vanilla	5 ml
½ to ¾ cup powdered sugar	120-180 ml

- Preheat oven to 350°(176° C).
- Empty contents of jar into large mixing bowl.
- Add butter, water and vanilla to dry ingredients and mix well.
- Dough will be crumbly at first but will hold its shape as you cut butter in.
- Take small pieces of dough and shape into crescents. (To make crescent shapes, roll pieces of dough into 3-inch (8 cm) lengths, place on sprayed baking sheet and shape into half moon, flattening top slightly.
- Bake for 12 to 14 minutes or until cookies are light brown around edges.
- While still warm, coat with powdered sugar. (An easy way to do this is to put cookies in resealable plastic bag with about ½ cup (120 ml) powdered sugar. Seal bag and gently shake to coat.)

www.cookbookresources.com

Nutty Crescents

Instructions for baking:

1 cup (2 sticks) butter, softened	240 ml
2 teaspoons cold water	10 ml
1 teaspoon vanilla	5 ml
½ to ¾ cup powdered sugar	120-180 ml

- Preheat oven to 350°(176° C).
- Empty contents of jar into large mixing bowl.
- Add butter, water and vanilla to dry ingredients and mix well.
- Dough will be crumbly at first but will hold its shape as you cut butter in.
- Take small pieces of dough and shape into crescents. (To make crescent shapes, roll pieces of dough into 3-inch (8 cm) lengths, place on sprayed baking sheet and shape into half moon, flattening top slightly.
- Bake for 12 to 14 minutes or until cookies are light brown around edges.
- While still warm, coat with powdered sugar. (An easy way to do this is to put cookies in resealable plastic bag with about ½ cup (120 ml) powdered sugar. Seal bag and gently shake to coat.)

www.cookbookresources.com

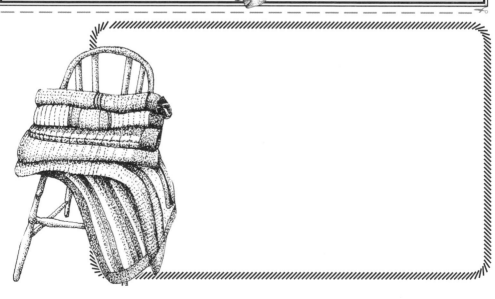

Nutty Crescents

Instructions for baking:

1 cup (2 sticks) butter, softened	240 ml
2 teaspoons cold water	10 ml
1 teaspoon vanilla	5 ml
½ to ¾ cup powdered sugar	120-180 ml

- Preheat oven to 350°(176° C).
- Empty contents of jar into large mixing bowl.
- Add butter, water and vanilla to dry ingredients and mix well.
- Dough will be crumbly at first but will hold its shape as you cut butter in.
- Take small pieces of dough and shape into crescents. (To make crescent shapes, roll pieces of dough into 3-inch (8 cm) lengths, place on sprayed baking sheet and shape into half moon, flattening top slightly.
- Bake for 12 to 14 minutes or until cookies are light brown around edges.
- While still warm, coat with powdered sugar. (An easy way to do this is to put cookies in resealable plastic bag with about ½ cup (120 ml) powdered sugar. Seal bag and gently shake to coat.)   www.cookbookresources.com

Nutty Crescents

Instructions for baking:

1 cup (2 sticks) butter, softened	240 ml
2 teaspoons cold water	10 ml
1 teaspoon vanilla	5 ml
½ to ¾ cup powdered sugar	120-180 ml

- Preheat oven to 350°(176° C).
- Empty contents of jar into large mixing bowl.
- Add butter, water and vanilla to dry ingredients and mix well.
- Dough will be crumbly at first but will hold its shape as you cut butter in.
- Take small pieces of dough and shape into crescents. (To make crescent shapes, roll pieces of dough into 3-inch (8 cm) lengths, place on sprayed baking sheet and shape into half moon, flattening top slightly.
- Bake for 12 to 14 minutes or until cookies are light brown around edges.
- While still warm, coat with powdered sugar. (An easy way to do this is to put cookies in resealable plastic bag with about ½ cup (120 ml) powdered sugar. Seal bag and gently shake to coat.)   www.cookbookresources.com

Nutty Crescents

Instructions for baking:

1 cup (2 sticks) butter, softened	240 ml
2 teaspoons cold water	10 ml
1 teaspoon vanilla	5 ml
½ to ¾ cup powdered sugar	120-180 ml

- Preheat oven to 350°(176° C).
- Empty contents of jar into large mixing bowl.
- Add butter, water and vanilla to dry ingredients and mix well.
- Dough will be crumbly at first but will hold its shape as you cut butter in.
- Take small pieces of dough and shape into crescents. (To make crescent shapes, roll pieces of dough into 3-inch (8 cm) lengths, place on sprayed baking sheet and shape into half moon, flattening top slightly.
- Bake for 12 to 14 minutes or until cookies are light brown around edges.
- While still warm, coat with powdered sugar. (An easy way to do this is to put cookies in resealable plastic bag with about ½ cup (120 ml) powdered sugar. Seal bag and gently shake to coat.)   www.cookbookresources.com

Classic Shortbread

Classic Shortbread

Shortbread is one of the simplest, yet most delicious cookie recipes you can make. It's delicate and tender and has a flavor that can't be resisted. One jar makes three batches of shortbread, meaning your gift can be used more than once.

Ingredients for jar:

3 cups flour	710 ml
1 cup powdered sugar	240 ml
½ teaspoon salt	2 ml

Instructions for jar:

■ Combine flour, sugar and salt. Spoon into 1-quart (1 L) jar.

♥ *Decorate jar using the suggestions and tips found on pages 4 and 5.*

Classic Shortbread

One jar of dry ingredients makes three batches.
The instructions are for one batch.

Instructions for baking:

¹/₃ mixture from jar
½ cup (1 stick) butter at room temperature   120 ml
¼ teaspoon vanilla   1 ml

- Preheat oven to 325° (162°C).

- Place butter and vanilla in medium bowl and stir in one-third mixture from jar, a little at a time, until all ingredients blend. (A wooden spoon works well for mixing this stiff dough.)

- Turn mixture out onto lightly floured surface and knead lightly until smooth. (Don't overwork dough.)

- Pat dough out into ¼-inch (.6 cm) thick circle on ungreased baking pan.

- Cut dough circle into 8 equal wedges, like a pie, and prick entire surface with fork.

- Bake for 20 to 25 minutes until shortbread is very light brown. Remove from oven and cool for about 10 minutes before cutting pieces apart with sharp knife.

"The road to a friend's house is never long."
- Danish Proverb

Classic Shortbread
One jar of dry ingredients makes three batches. The instructions are for one batch.

Instructions for baking:

¹/₃ mixture from jar	
½ cup (1 stick) butter at room temperature	**120 ml**
¼ teaspoon vanilla	**1 ml**

- Preheat oven to 325°(162°C).
- Place butter and vanilla in medium bowl and stir in one-third mixture from jar, a little at a time, until all ingredients blend. (A wooden spoon works well for mixing this stiff dough.)
- Turn mixture out onto lightly floured surface and knead lightly until smooth. (Don't overwork dough.)
- Pat dough out into ¼-inch (.6 cm) thick circle on ungreased baking pan.
- Cut dough circle into 8 equal wedges, like a pie, and prick entire surface with fork.
- Bake for 20 to 25 minutes until shortbread is very light brown. Remove from oven and cool for about 10 minutes before cutting pieces apart with sharp knife.

www.cookbookresources.com

- ✂

Classic Shortbread
One jar of dry ingredients makes three batches. The instructions are for one batch.

Instructions for baking:

¹/₃ mixture from jar	
½ cup (1 stick) butter at room temperature	**120 ml**
¼ teaspoon vanilla	**1 ml**

- Preheat oven to 325°(162°C).
- Place butter and vanilla in medium bowl and stir in one-third mixture from jar, a little at a time, until all ingredients blend. (A wooden spoon works well for mixing this stiff dough.)
- Turn mixture out onto lightly floured surface and knead lightly until smooth. (Don't overwork dough.)
- Pat dough out into ¼-inch (.6 cm) thick circle on ungreased baking pan.
- Cut dough circle into 8 equal wedges, like a pie, and prick entire surface with fork.
- Bake for 20 to 25 minutes until shortbread is very light brown. Remove from oven and cool for about 10 minutes before cutting pieces apart with sharp knife.

www.cookbookresources.com

- ✂

Classic Shortbread
One jar of dry ingredients makes three batches. The instructions are for one batch.

Instructions for baking:

¹/₃ mixture from jar	
½ cup (1 stick) butter at room temperature	**120 ml**
¼ teaspoon vanilla	**1 ml**

- Preheat oven to 325°(162°C).
- Place butter and vanilla in medium bowl and stir in one-third mixture from jar, a little at a time, until all ingredients blend. (A wooden spoon works well for mixing this stiff dough.)
- Turn mixture out onto lightly floured surface and knead lightly until smooth. (Don't overwork dough.)
- Pat dough out into ¼-inch (.6 cm) thick circle on ungreased baking pan.
- Cut dough circle into 8 equal wedges, like a pie, and prick entire surface with fork.
- Bake for 20 to 25 minutes until shortbread is very light brown. Remove from oven and cool for about 10 minutes before cutting pieces apart with sharp knife.

www.cookbookresources.com

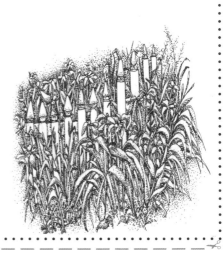

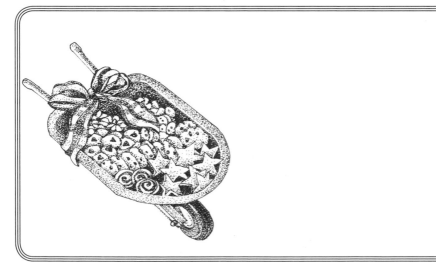

Classic Shortbread

One jar of dry ingredients makes three batches. The instructions are for one batch.

Instructions for baking:

⅓ mixture from jar
½ cup (1 stick) butter at room temperature   120 ml
¼ teaspoon vanilla   1 ml

- Preheat oven to 325°(162°C).
- Place butter and vanilla in medium bowl and stir in one-third mixture from jar, a little at a time, until all ingredients blend. (A wooden spoon works well for mixing this stiff dough.)
- Turn mixture out onto lightly floured surface and knead lightly until smooth. (Don't overwork dough.)
- Pat dough out into ¼-inch (.6 cm) thick circle on ungreased baking pan.
- Cut dough circle into 8 equal wedges, like a pie, and prick entire surface with fork.
- Bake for 20 to 25 minutes until shortbread is very light brown. Remove from oven and cool for about 10 minutes before cutting pieces apart with sharp knife.

www.cookbookresources.com

Classic Shortbread

One jar of dry ingredients makes three batches. The instructions are for one batch.

Instructions for baking:

⅓ mixture from jar
½ cup (1 stick) butter at room temperature   120 ml
¼ teaspoon vanilla   1 ml

- Preheat oven to 325°(162°C).
- Place butter and vanilla in medium bowl and stir in one-third mixture from jar, a little at a time, until all ingredients blend. (A wooden spoon works well for mixing this stiff dough.)
- Turn mixture out onto lightly floured surface and knead lightly until smooth. (Don't overwork dough.)
- Pat dough out into ¼-inch (.6 cm) thick circle on ungreased baking pan.
- Cut dough circle into 8 equal wedges, like a pie, and prick entire surface with fork.
- Bake for 20 to 25 minutes until shortbread is very light brown. Remove from oven and cool for about 10 minutes before cutting pieces apart with sharp knife.

www.cookbookresources.com

Classic Shortbread

One jar of dry ingredients makes three batches. The instructions are for one batch.

Instructions for baking:

⅓ mixture from jar
½ cup (1 stick) butter at room temperature   120 ml
¼ teaspoon vanilla   1 ml

- Preheat oven to 325°(162°C).
- Place butter and vanilla in medium bowl and stir in one-third mixture from jar, a little at a time, until all ingredients blend. (A wooden spoon works well for mixing this stiff dough.)
- Turn mixture out onto lightly floured surface and knead lightly until smooth. (Don't overwork dough.)
- Pat dough out into ¼-inch (.6 cm) thick circle on ungreased baking pan.
- Cut dough circle into 8 equal wedges, like a pie, and prick entire surface with fork.
- Bake for 20 to 25 minutes until shortbread is very light brown. Remove from oven and cool for about 10 minutes before cutting pieces apart with sharp knife.

www.cookbookresources.com

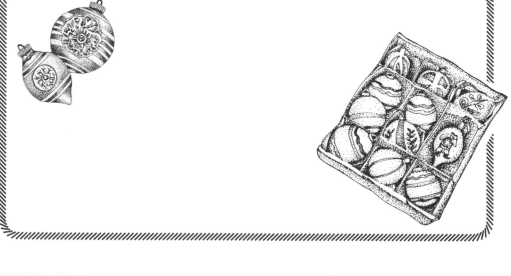

Chocolate-Almond Biscotti

Chocolate-Almond Biscotti

Ingredients for jar:

1¼ cups sugar	300 ml
¼ cup unsweetened cocoa powder	60 ml
2¼ cups flour	540 ml
1 teaspoon baking powder	5 ml
¼ teaspoon salt	1 ml
½ cup chopped almonds	120 ml

Instructions for jar:

- Spoon sugar into 1-quart (1 L) jar and then spoon cocoa powder over sugar.

- Combine flour, baking powder and salt. Spoon over cocoa powder.

- Spoon almonds over flour and press gently to fit.

♥ *Decorate jar using the suggestions and tips found on pages 4 and 5.*

Chocolate-Almond Biscotti

Instructions for baking:

2 eggs
1 teaspoon almond extract   **5 ml**
½ cup (1 stick) butter, softened   **120 ml**

■ Preheat oven to 350° (176° C).

■ In large mixing bowl, beat eggs with almond extract and butter.

■ Add contents of jar, a little at a time, to butter mixture and stir well after each addition. (Dough will be stiff.)

■ Divide dough in half. Shape each half into log about 12 inches long. Place both logs on sprayed baking sheet and bake for 30 minutes or until logs set.

■ Remove from oven and cool on baking sheet for 10 minutes. Use sharp, serrated knife to cut each log diagonally into ½-inch (1.2 cm) slices.

■ Place slices on baking sheets and bake for another 7 minutes. Turn each slice over and bake for another 7 to 8 minutes.

■ Remove from oven and cool.

"We make a living by what we get, but we make a life by what we give."

- Winston Churchill

Chocolate-Almond Biscotti

Instructions for baking:

2 eggs	
1 teaspoon almond extract	**5 ml**
½ cup (1 stick) butter, softened	**120 ml**

- Preheat oven to 350° (176° C).
- In large mixing bowl, beat eggs with almond extract and butter.
- Add contents of jar, a little at a time, to butter mixture and stir well after each addition. (Dough will be stiff.)
- Divide dough in half. Shape each half into log about 12 inches (30 cm) long. Place both logs on sprayed baking sheet and bake for 30 minutes or until logs set.
- Remove from oven and cool on baking sheet for 10 minutes. Use sharp, serrated knife to cut each log diagonally into ½-inch (1.2 cm) slices.
- Place slices on baking sheets and bake for another 7 minutes. Turn each slice over and bake for another 7 to 8 minutes.
- Remove from oven and cool.   www.cookbookresources.com

Chocolate-Almond Biscotti

Instructions for baking:

2 eggs	
1 teaspoon almond extract	**5 ml**
½ cup (1 stick) butter, softened	**120 ml**

- Preheat oven to 350° (176° C).
- In large mixing bowl, beat eggs with almond extract and butter.
- Add contents of jar, a little at a time, to butter mixture and stir well after each addition. (Dough will be stiff.)
- Divide dough in half. Shape each half into log about 12 inches (30 cm) long. Place both logs on sprayed baking sheet and bake for 30 minutes or until logs set.
- Remove from oven and cool on baking sheet for 10 minutes. Use sharp, serrated knife to cut each log diagonally into ½-inch (1.2 cm) slices.
- Place slices on baking sheets and bake for another 7 minutes. Turn each slice over and bake for another 7 to 8 minutes.
- Remove from oven and cool.   www.cookbookresources.com

Chocolate-Almond Biscotti

Instructions for baking:

2 eggs	
1 teaspoon almond extract	**5 ml**
½ cup (1 stick) butter, softened	**120 ml**

- Preheat oven to 350° (176° C).
- In large mixing bowl, beat eggs with almond extract and butter.
- Add contents of jar, a little at a time, to butter mixture and stir well after each addition. (Dough will be stiff.)
- Divide dough in half. Shape each half into log about 12 inches (30 cm) long. Place both logs on sprayed baking sheet and bake for 30 minutes or until logs set.
- Remove from oven and cool on baking sheet for 10 minutes. Use sharp, serrated knife to cut each log diagonally into ½-inch (1.2 cm) slices.
- Place slices on baking sheets and bake for another 7 minutes. Turn each slice over and bake for another 7 to 8 minutes.
- Remove from oven and cool.   www.cookbookresources.com

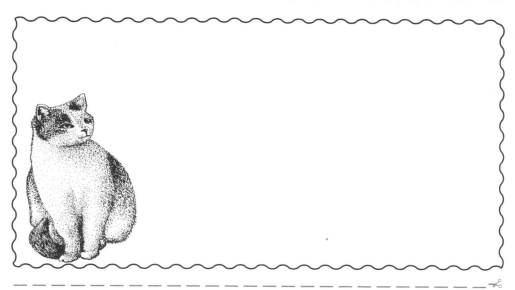

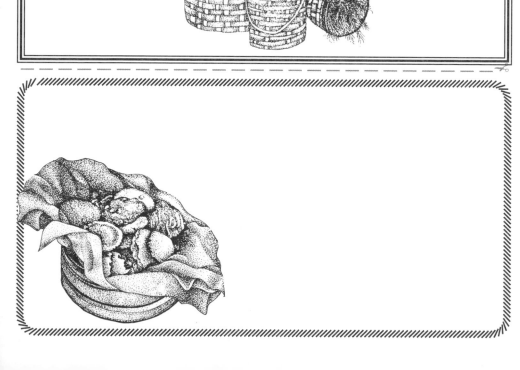

Chocolate-Almond Biscotti

Instructions for baking:

2 eggs
1 teaspoon almond extract   **5 ml**
½ cup (1 stick) butter, softened   **120 ml**

- Preheat oven to 350° (176° C).
- In large mixing bowl, beat eggs with almond extract and butter.
- Add contents of jar, a little at a time, to butter mixture and stir well after each addition. (Dough will be stiff.)
- Divide dough in half. Shape each half into log about 12 inches (30 cm) long. Place both logs on sprayed baking sheet and bake for 30 minutes or until logs set.
- Remove from oven and cool on baking sheet for 10 minutes. Use sharp, serrated knife to cut each log diagonally into ½-inch (1.2 cm) slices.
- Place slices on baking sheets and bake for another 7 minutes. Turn each slice over and bake for another 7 to 8 minutes.
- Remove from oven and cool.   www.cookbookresources.com

Chocolate-Almond Biscotti

Instructions for baking:

2 eggs
1 teaspoon almond extract   **5 ml**
½ cup (1 stick) butter, softened   **120 ml**

- Preheat oven to 350° (176° C).
- In large mixing bowl, beat eggs with almond extract and butter.
- Add contents of jar, a little at a time, to butter mixture and stir well after each addition. (Dough will be stiff.)
- Divide dough in half. Shape each half into log about 12 inches (30 cm) long. Place both logs on sprayed baking sheet and bake for 30 minutes or until logs set.
- Remove from oven and cool on baking sheet for 10 minutes. Use sharp, serrated knife to cut each log diagonally into ½-inch (1.2 cm) slices.
- Place slices on baking sheets and bake for another 7 minutes. Turn each slice over and bake for another 7 to 8 minutes.
- Remove from oven and cool.   www.cookbookresources.com

Chocolate-Almond Biscotti

Instructions for baking:

2 eggs
1 teaspoon almond extract   **5 ml**
½ cup (1 stick) butter, softened   **120 ml**

- Preheat oven to 350° (176° C).
- In large mixing bowl, beat eggs with almond extract and butter.
- Add contents of jar, a little at a time, to butter mixture and stir well after each addition. (Dough will be stiff.)
- Divide dough in half. Shape each half into log about 12 inches (30 cm) long. Place both logs on sprayed baking sheet and bake for 30 minutes or until logs set.
- Remove from oven and cool on baking sheet for 10 minutes. Use sharp, serrated knife to cut each log diagonally into ½-inch (1.2 cm) slices.
- Place slices on baking sheets and bake for another 7 minutes. Turn each slice over and bake for another 7 to 8 minutes.
- Remove from oven and cool.   www.cookbookresources.com

Spiced Biscotti

Spiced Biscotti

Ingredients for jar:

2 cups flour	480 ml
2 teaspoons cinnamon	10 ml
1 tablespoon ground ginger	15 ml
1 teaspoon ground cloves	5 ml
½ teaspoon baking powder	2 ml
1 cup quick-cooking oats	240 ml
1 cup sugar	240 ml
¼ cup finely chopped pecans	10 ml

Instructions for jar:

- Combine flour with cinnamon, ginger, cloves and baking powder. Spoon into 1-quart (1 L) jar.

- Spoon oats over flour and spoon sugar over oats.

- Add pecans on top of sugar and press down lightly to fit into jar.

Tip: Almonds or walnuts work well too.

Spiced Biscotti

Instructions for baking:

½ **cup (1 stick) butter, very soft**	**120 ml**
2 eggs, beaten	
1 teaspoon vanilla	**5 ml**

- Preheat oven to 350° (176° C).

- Whisk butter, eggs and vanilla together in large mixing bowl.

- Slowly add jar contents and mix after each addition until dough holds its shape.

- Divide dough in half and shape each half into 12-inch (30 cm) long roll.

- Place both rolls on ungreased baking sheet.

- Bake for 25 minutes or until light brown.

- Cut each roll diagonally into slices ½-inch (1.2 cm) thick using sharp, serrated knife.

- Place slices on ungreased baking sheet and bake for 7 minutes. Turn each slice over and bake for 7 or 8 more minutes or until slices are light brown.

- Move to cooling rack.

> *"The function of wisdom is to discriminate between good and evil."*
> *- Cicero*

Spiced Biscotti

Instructions for baking:

½ cup (1 stick) butter, very soft	120 ml
2 eggs, beaten	
1 teaspoon vanilla	5 ml

- Preheat oven to 350° (176° C).
- Whisk butter, eggs and vanilla together in large mixing bowl.
- Slowly add jar contents and mix after each addition until dough holds its shape.
- Divide dough in half and shape each half into 12-inch (30 cm) long roll.
- Place both rolls on ungreased baking sheet.
- Bake for 25 minutes or until light brown.
- Cut each roll diagonally into slices ½-inch (1.2 cm) thick using sharp, serrated knife.
- Place slices on ungreased baking sheet and bake for 7 minutes. Turn each slice over and bake for 7 or 8 more minutes or until slices are light brown.
- Move to cooling rack.   www.cookbookresources.com

Spiced Biscotti

Instructions for baking:

½ cup (1 stick) butter, very soft	120 ml
2 eggs, beaten	
1 teaspoon vanilla	5 ml

- Preheat oven to 350° (176° C).
- Whisk butter, eggs and vanilla together in large mixing bowl.
- Slowly add jar contents and mix after each addition until dough holds its shape.
- Divide dough in half and shape each half into 12-inch (30 cm) long roll.
- Place both rolls on ungreased baking sheet.
- Bake for 25 minutes or until light brown.
- Cut each roll diagonally into slices ½-inch (1.2 cm) thick using sharp, serrated knife.
- Place slices on ungreased baking sheet and bake for 7 minutes. Turn each slice over and bake for 7 or 8 more minutes or until slices are light brown.
- Move to cooling rack.   www.cookbookresources.com

Spiced Biscotti

Instructions for baking:

½ cup (1 stick) butter, very soft	120 ml
2 eggs, beaten	
1 teaspoon vanilla	5 ml

- Preheat oven to 350° (176° C).
- Whisk butter, eggs and vanilla together in large mixing bowl.
- Slowly add jar contents and mix after each addition until dough holds its shape.
- Divide dough in half and shape each half into 12-inch (30 cm) long roll.
- Place both rolls on ungreased baking sheet.
- Bake for 25 minutes or until light brown.
- Cut each roll diagonally into slices ½-inch (1.2 cm) thick using sharp, serrated knife.
- Place slices on ungreased baking sheet and bake for 7 minutes. Turn each slice over and bake for 7 or 8 more minutes or until slices are light brown.
- Move to cooling rack.   www.cookbookresources.com

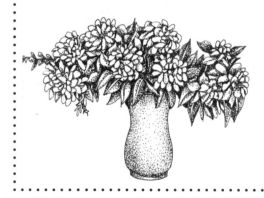

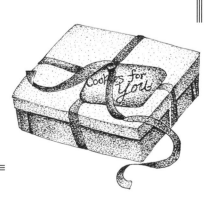

Spiced Biscotti

Instructions for baking:

½ cup (1 stick) butter, very soft	**120 ml**
2 eggs, beaten	
1 teaspoon vanilla	**5 ml**

- Preheat oven to 350° (176° C).
- Whisk butter, eggs and vanilla together in large mixing bowl.
- Slowly add jar contents and mix after each addition until dough holds its shape.
- Divide dough in half and shape each half into 12-inch (30 cm) long roll.
- Place both rolls on ungreased baking sheet.
- Bake for 25 minutes or until light brown.
- Cut each roll diagonally into slices ½-inch (1.2 cm) thick using sharp, serrated knife.
- Place slices on ungreased baking sheet and bake for 7 minutes. Turn each slice over and bake for 7 or 8 more minutes or until slices are light brown.
- Move to cooling rack.

www.cookbookresources.com

Spiced Biscotti

Instructions for baking:

½ cup (1 stick) butter, very soft	**120 ml**
2 eggs, beaten	
1 teaspoon vanilla	**5 ml**

- Preheat oven to 350° (176° C).
- Whisk butter, eggs and vanilla together in large mixing bowl.
- Slowly add jar contents and mix after each addition until dough holds its shape.
- Divide dough in half and shape each half into 12-inch (30 cm) long roll.
- Place both rolls on ungreased baking sheet.
- Bake for 25 minutes or until light brown.
- Cut each roll diagonally into slices ½-inch (1.2 cm) thick using sharp, serrated knife.
- Place slices on ungreased baking sheet and bake for 7 minutes. Turn each slice over and bake for 7 or 8 more minutes or until slices are light brown.
- Move to cooling rack.

www.cookbookresources.com

Spiced Biscotti

Instructions for baking:

½ cup (1 stick) butter, very soft	**120 ml**
2 eggs, beaten	
1 teaspoon vanilla	**5 ml**

- Preheat oven to 350° (176° C).
- Whisk butter, eggs and vanilla together in large mixing bowl.
- Slowly add jar contents and mix after each addition until dough holds its shape.
- Divide dough in half and shape each half into 12-inch (30 cm) long roll.
- Place both rolls on ungreased baking sheet.
- Bake for 25 minutes or until light brown.
- Cut each roll diagonally into slices ½-inch (1.2 cm) thick using sharp, serrated knife.
- Place slices on ungreased baking sheet and bake for 7 minutes. Turn each slice over and bake for 7 or 8 more minutes or until slices are light brown.
- Move to cooling rack.

www.cookbookresources.com

Molasses Bars

Molasses Bars

Ingredients for jar:

1 cup packed brown sugar	240 ml
3 cups flour	210 ml
1 tablespoon baking powder	15 ml
2 teaspoons ground ginger	10 ml
1 teaspoon salt	5 ml
½ teaspoon baking soda	2 ml
¼ cup raisins	60 ml

Instructions for jar:

- Spoon brown sugar into 1-quart (1 L) jar.

- Combine flour, baking powder, ginger, salt and baking soda. Spoon over brown sugar.

- Put raisins on top and press gently to fit.

♥ *Decorate jar using the suggestions and tips found on pages 4 and 5.*

Molasses Bars

Instructions for baking:

1 cup (2 sticks) butter, softened	**240 ml**
1 cup molasses	**240 ml**
2 eggs, beaten	
²/₃ cup milk	**160 ml**

- Preheat oven to 350° (176° C).

- Beat butter, molasses, eggs and milk together in large mixing bowl.

- Slowly add ingredients from jar and stir well after each addition.

- Spread batter in sprayed 9 x 13-inch (23 x 33 cm) baking pan.

- Bake for 20 to 25 minutes.

- When cool, cut into rectangles about 1½ inches wide x 3 inches long (3.5 x 8 cm).

"Common sense is the knack of seeing things as they are and doing things as they ought to be done."

- Harriet Beecher Stowe

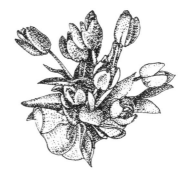

Molasses Bars

Instructions for baking:

1 cup (2 sticks) butter, softened	240 ml
1 cup molasses	240 ml
2 eggs, beaten	
2/3 cup milk	160 ml

- Preheat oven to 350°(176° C).
- Beat butter, molasses, eggs and milk together in large mixing bowl.
- Slowly add ingredients from jar and stir well after each addition.

- Spread batter in sprayed 9 x 13-inch (23 x 33 cm) baking pan.
- Bake for 20 to 25 minutes.

- When cool, cut into rectangles about 1½ inches (3.5 cm) wide x 3 inches (8 cm) long.

www.cookbookresources.com

Molasses Bars

Instructions for baking:

1 cup (2 sticks) butter, softened	240 ml
1 cup molasses	240 ml
2 eggs, beaten	
2/3 cup milk	160 ml

- Preheat oven to 350°(176° C).
- Beat butter, molasses, eggs and milk together in large mixing bowl.
- Slowly add ingredients from jar and stir well after each addition.

- Spread batter in sprayed 9 x 13-inch (23 x 33 cm) baking pan.
- Bake for 20 to 25 minutes.

- When cool, cut into rectangles about 1½ inches (3.5 cm) wide x 3 inches (8 cm) long.

www.cookbookresources.com

Molasses Bars

Instructions for baking:

1 cup (2 sticks) butter, softened	240 ml
1 cup molasses	240 ml
2 eggs, beaten	
2/3 cup milk	160 ml

- Preheat oven to 350°(176° C).
- Beat butter, molasses, eggs and milk together in large mixing bowl.
- Slowly add ingredients from jar and stir well after each addition.

- Spread batter in sprayed 9 x 13-inch (23 x 33 cm) baking pan.
- Bake for 20 to 25 minutes.

- When cool, cut into rectangles about 1½ inches (3.5 cm) wide x 3 inches (8 cm) long.

www.cookbookresources.com

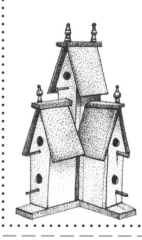

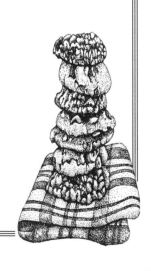

Molasses Bars

Instructions for baking:

1 cup (2 sticks) butter, softened	240 ml
1 cup molasses	240 ml
2 eggs, beaten	
2/3 cup milk	160 ml

- Preheat oven to 350°(176° C).
- Beat butter, molasses, eggs and milk together in large mixing bowl.
- Slowly add ingredients from jar and stir well after each addition.
- Spread batter in sprayed 9 x 13-inch (23 x 33 cm) baking pan.
- Bake for 20 to 25 minutes.
- When cool, cut into rectangles about 1½ inches (3.5 cm) wide x 3 inches (8 cm) long.

www.cookbookresources.com

- ✂

Molasses Bars

Instructions for baking:

1 cup (2 sticks) butter, softened	240 ml
1 cup molasses	240 ml
2 eggs, beaten	
2/3 cup milk	160 ml

- Preheat oven to 350°(176° C).
- Beat butter, molasses, eggs and milk together in large mixing bowl.
- Slowly add ingredients from jar and stir well after each addition.
- Spread batter in sprayed 9 x 13-inch (23 x 33 cm) baking pan.
- Bake for 20 to 25 minutes.
- When cool, cut into rectangles about 1½ inches (3.5 cm) wide x 3 inches (8 cm) long.

www.cookbookresources.com

- ✂

Molasses Bars

Instructions for baking:

1 cup (2 sticks) butter, softened	240 ml
1 cup molasses	240 ml
2 eggs, beaten	
2/3 cup milk	160 ml

- Preheat oven to 350°(176° C).
- Beat butter, molasses, eggs and milk together in large mixing bowl.
- Slowly add ingredients from jar and stir well after each addition.
- Spread batter in sprayed 9 x 13-inch (23 x 33 cm) baking pan.
- Bake for 20 to 25 minutes.
- When cool, cut into rectangles about 1½ inches (3.5 cm) wide x 3 inches (8 cm) long.

www.cookbookresources.com

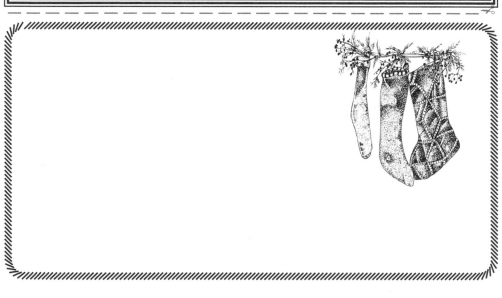

Apricot Squares

Apricot Squares

Ingredients for jar:

1½ cups flour	360 ml
1 teaspoon baking powder	5 ml
1¼ teaspoons salt	
½ cup packed brown sugar	120 ml
½ cup sugar	120 ml
1½ cups quick-cooking oats	360 ml
¼ cup finely chopped almonds	60 ml

Instructions for jar:

- Combine flour, baking powder and salt. Spoon into 1-quart (1 L) jar.

- Spoon brown sugar over flour mixture.

- Layer sugar, oats and almonds over brown sugar.

♥ *Decorate jar using the suggestions and tips found on pages 4 and 5.*

Apricot Squares

Instructions for baking:

¾ cup (1½ sticks) butter, softened 180 ml
¾ cup apricot preserves 180 ml

- Preheat oven to 375° (190°C).

- Empty contents of jar into large mixing bowl. Stir to thoroughly mix dry ingredients.

- Cut butter into dry ingredients until mixture is crumbly.

- Press two-thirds crumb mixture into sprayed 9 x 9-inch (23 x 23 cm) baking pan.

- Spread preserves evenly over crumb mixture in pan.

- Sprinkle remaining crumb mixture over preserves.

- Bake for 30 to 35 minutes or until top is nicely brown. Remove from oven, cool and cut into squares.

"It is a happy talent to know how to play."
- Ralph Waldo Emerson

Apricot Squares

Instructions for baking:

¾ cup (1½ sticks) butter, softened	**180 ml**
¾ cup apricot preserves	**180 ml**

- Preheat oven to 375° (190°C).
- Empty contents of jar into large mixing bowl. Stir to thoroughly mix dry ingredients.
- Cut butter into dry ingredients until mixture is crumbly.
- Press two-thirds crumb mixture into sprayed 9 x 9-inch (23 x 23 cm) baking pan.
- Spread preserves evenly over crumb mixture in pan.
- Sprinkle remaining crumb mixture over preserves.
- Bake for 30 to 35 minutes or until top is nicely brown. Remove from oven, cool and cut into squares.

www.cookbookresources.com

- ✂

Apricot Squares

Instructions for baking:

¾ cup (1½ sticks) butter, softened	**180 ml**
¾ cup apricot preserves	**180 ml**

- Preheat oven to 375° (190°C).
- Empty contents of jar into large mixing bowl. Stir to thoroughly mix dry ingredients.
- Cut butter into dry ingredients until mixture is crumbly.
- Press two-thirds crumb mixture into sprayed 9 x 9-inch (23 x 23 cm) baking pan.
- Spread preserves evenly over crumb mixture in pan.
- Sprinkle remaining crumb mixture over preserves.
- Bake for 30 to 35 minutes or until top is nicely brown. Remove from oven, cool and cut into squares.

www.cookbookresources.com

- ✂

Apricot Squares

Instructions for baking:

¾ cup (1½ sticks) butter, softened	**180 ml**
¾ cup apricot preserves	**180 ml**

- Preheat oven to 375° (190°C).
- Empty contents of jar into large mixing bowl. Stir to thoroughly mix dry ingredients.
- Cut butter into dry ingredients until mixture is crumbly.
- Press two-thirds crumb mixture into sprayed 9 x 9-inch (23 x 23 cm) baking pan.
- Spread preserves evenly over crumb mixture in pan.
- Sprinkle remaining crumb mixture over preserves.
- Bake for 30 to 35 minutes or until top is nicely brown. Remove from oven, cool and cut into squares.

www.cookbookresources.com

Apricot Squares

Instructions for baking:

¾ cup (1½ sticks) butter, softened	**180 ml**
¾ cup apricot preserves	**180 ml**

- Preheat oven to 375° (190°C).
- Empty contents of jar into large mixing bowl. Stir to thoroughly mix dry ingredients.
- Cut butter into dry ingredients until mixture is crumbly.
- Press two-thirds crumb mixture into sprayed 9 x 9-inch (23 x 23 cm) baking pan.
- Spread preserves evenly over crumb mixture in pan.
- Sprinkle remaining crumb mixture over preserves.
- Bake for 30 to 35 minutes or until top is nicely brown. Remove from oven, cool and cut into squares.

www.cookbookresources.com

Apricot Squares

Instructions for baking:

¾ cup (1½ sticks) butter, softened	**180 ml**
¾ cup apricot preserves	**180 ml**

- Preheat oven to 375° (190°C).
- Empty contents of jar into large mixing bowl. Stir to thoroughly mix dry ingredients.
- Cut butter into dry ingredients until mixture is crumbly.
- Press two-thirds crumb mixture into sprayed 9 x 9-inch (23 x 23 cm) baking pan.
- Spread preserves evenly over crumb mixture in pan.
- Sprinkle remaining crumb mixture over preserves.
- Bake for 30 to 35 minutes or until top is nicely brown. Remove from oven, cool and cut into squares.

www.cookbookresources.com

Apricot Squares

Instructions for baking:

¾ cup (1½ sticks) butter, softened	**180 ml**
¾ cup apricot preserves	**180 ml**

- Preheat oven to 375° (190°C).
- Empty contents of jar into large mixing bowl. Stir to thoroughly mix dry ingredients.
- Cut butter into dry ingredients until mixture is crumbly.
- Press two-thirds crumb mixture into sprayed 9 x 9-inch (23 x 23 cm) baking pan.
- Spread preserves evenly over crumb mixture in pan.
- Sprinkle remaining crumb mixture over preserves.
- Bake for 30 to 35 minutes or until top is nicely brown. Remove from oven, cool and cut into squares.

www.cookbookresources.com

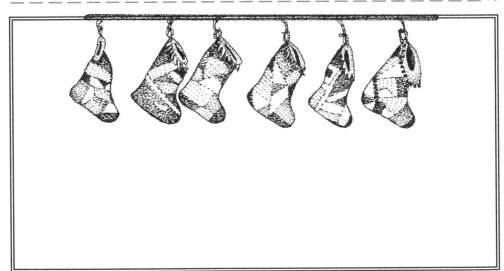

Strawberry Crispy Squares

Strawberry Crispy Squares

This recipe would make a great gift if placed in a basket with a jar of gourmet strawberry jam and a pretty set of oven mitts.

Ingredients for jar:

1½ cups flour	360 ml
1 teaspoon baking powder	5 ml
¼ teaspoon salt	1 ml
1¼ cups packed brown sugar	300 ml
1½ cups quick-cooking oats	360 ml

Instructions for jar:

- Combine flour, baking powder and salt. Spoon into 1-quart (1 L) jar.

- Spoon brown sugar over flour mixture.

- Spoon oats over brown sugar.

♥ *Decorate jar using the suggestions and tips found on pages 4 and 5.*

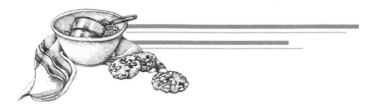

Strawberry Crispy Squares

Instructions for baking:

¾ cup (1½ sticks) butter, softened	**180 ml**
1¼ cups strawberry jam	**300 ml**

- Preheat oven to 350°(176°C).

- Empty contents of jar into large mixing bowl.

- Cut butter into dry ingredients until mixture is crumbly.

- Press two-thirds crumb mixture evenly into sprayed 9 x 13-inch (23 x 33 cm) baking pan.

- Spread jam evenly over crumb mixture and sprinkle remaining crumb mixture on top.

- Bake for 35 minutes. Cool before cutting into squares.

"The best thing you can wear is a smile."
- Grandma Mullins

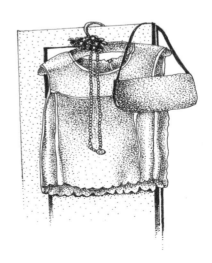

Strawberry Crispy Squares

Instructions for baking:

¾ cup (1½ sticks) butter, softened	**180 ml**
1¼ cups strawberry jam	**300 ml**

- Preheat oven to 350° (176°).
- Empty contents of jar into large mixing bowl.
- Cut butter into dry ingredients until mixture is crumbly.
- Press two-thirds crumb mixture evenly into sprayed 9 x 13-inch (23 x 33 cm) baking pan.
- Spread jam evenly over crumb mixture and sprinkle remaining crumb mixture on top.
- Bake for 35 minutes. Cool before cutting into squares.

www.cookbookresources.com

Strawberry Crispy Squares

Instructions for baking:

¾ cup (1½ sticks) butter, softened	**180 ml**
1¼ cups strawberry jam	**300 ml**

- Preheat oven to 350° (176°).
- Empty contents of jar into large mixing bowl.
- Cut butter into dry ingredients until mixture is crumbly.
- Press two-thirds crumb mixture evenly into sprayed 9 x 13-inch (23 x 33 cm) baking pan.
- Spread jam evenly over crumb mixture and sprinkle remaining crumb mixture on top.
- Bake for 35 minutes. Cool before cutting into squares.

www.cookbookresources.com

Strawberry Crispy Squares

Instructions for baking:

¾ cup (1½ sticks) butter, softened	**180 ml**
1¼ cups strawberry jam	**300 ml**

- Preheat oven to 350° (176°).
- Empty contents of jar into large mixing bowl.
- Cut butter into dry ingredients until mixture is crumbly.
- Press two-thirds crumb mixture evenly into sprayed 9 x 13-inch (23 x 33 cm) baking pan.
- Spread jam evenly over crumb mixture and sprinkle remaining crumb mixture on top.
- Bake for 35 minutes. Cool before cutting into squares.

www.cookbookresources.com

Strawberry Crispy Squares

Instructions for baking:

¾ cup (1½ sticks) butter, softened	**180 ml**
1¼ cups strawberry jam	**300 ml**

- Preheat oven to 350° (176°).
- Empty contents of jar into large mixing bowl.
- Cut butter into dry ingredients until mixture is crumbly.
- Press two-thirds crumb mixture evenly into sprayed 9 x 13-inch (23 x 33 cm) baking pan.
- Spread jam evenly over crumb mixture and sprinkle remaining crumb mixture on top.
- Bake for 35 minutes. Cool before cutting into squares.

www.cookbookresources.com

- ✂

Strawberry Crispy Squares

Instructions for baking:

¾ cup (1½ sticks) butter, softened	**180 ml**
1¼ cups strawberry jam	**300 ml**

- Preheat oven to 350° (176°).
- Empty contents of jar into large mixing bowl.
- Cut butter into dry ingredients until mixture is crumbly.
- Press two-thirds crumb mixture evenly into sprayed 9 x 13-inch (23 x 33 cm) baking pan.
- Spread jam evenly over crumb mixture and sprinkle remaining crumb mixture on top.
- Bake for 35 minutes. Cool before cutting into squares.

www.cookbookresources.com

- ✂

Strawberry Crispy Squares

Instructions for baking:

¾ cup (1½ sticks) butter, softened	**180 ml**
1¼ cups strawberry jam	**300 ml**

- Preheat oven to 350° (176°).
- Empty contents of jar into large mixing bowl.
- Cut butter into dry ingredients until mixture is crumbly.
- Press two-thirds crumb mixture evenly into sprayed 9 x 13-inch (23 x 33 cm) baking pan.
- Spread jam evenly over crumb mixture and sprinkle remaining crumb mixture on top.
- Bake for 35 minutes. Cool before cutting into squares.

www.cookbookresources.com

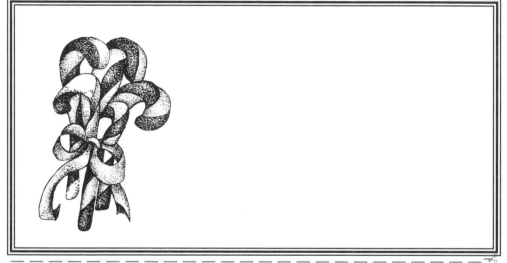

Frosted Butterscotch Bars

Frosted Butterscotch Bars

Ingredients for jar:

1½ cups packed brown sugar	360 ml
1½ cups flour	360 ml
1 tablespoon baking powder	15 ml
½ teaspoon salt	2 ml
¾ cup chopped pecans	180 ml
½ cup miniature chocolate chips	120 ml

Instructions for jar:

- Spoon brown sugar into 1-quart (1 L) jar.

- Combine flour, baking powder and salt. Spoon mixture over brown sugar.

- Layer pecans over flour mixture and chocolate chips over pecans.

♥ *Decorate jar using the suggestions and tips found on pages 4 and 5.*

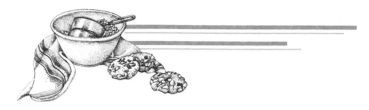

Frosted Butterscotch Bars

Instructions for baking:

½ cup (1 stick) butter, softened	**120 ml**
2 eggs	

- Preheat oven to 350° (176°C).
- Empty contents of jar into medium mixing bowl and stir to combine ingredients.
- Beat butter and eggs in large mixing bowl.
- Add dry ingredients to egg mixture in several additions and mix well after each.
- Spread batter in sprayed 9 x 13-inch (23 x 33 cm) baking pan.
- Bake for 20 to 25 minutes or until light brown on top.
- Remove from oven and cool. Frost with Chocolate Icing (recipe below) while warm.

Chocolate Icing:

¼ cup (½ stick) butter	60 ml
5 tablespoons cocoa powder	75 ml
¼ cup milk	60 ml
2 cups powdered sugar	480 ml
1 teaspoon vanilla	5 ml

- Melt butter in small saucepan over low heat.
- Stir in cocoa, milk and powdered sugar and mix well.
- Remove from heat and stir in vanilla and spread over warm bars.

Frosted Butterscotch Bars

Instructions for baking:

½ cup (1 stick) butter, softened	120 ml
2 eggs	

- Preheat oven to 350° (176°C).
- Empty contents of jar into medium mixing bowl and stir to combine ingredients.
- Beat butter and eggs in large mixing bowl.
- Add dry ingredients to egg mixture in several additions and mix well after each.
- Spread batter in sprayed 9 x 13-inch (23 x 33 cm) baking pan.
- Bake for 20 to 25 minutes or until light brown on top.
- Remove from oven and cool. Frost with Chocolate Icing while warm.

Chocolate Icing:

¼ cup (½ stick) butter	60 ml
5 tablespoons cocoa powder	75 ml
¼ cup milk	60 ml
2 cups powdered sugar	480 ml
1 teaspoon vanilla	5 ml

- Melt butter in small saucepan over low heat.
- Stir in cocoa, milk and powdered sugar and mix well.
- Remove from heat and stir in vanilla and spread over warm bars.

- ✂

Frosted Butterscotch Bars

Instructions for baking:

½ cup (1 stick) butter, softened	120 ml
2 eggs	

- Preheat oven to 350° (176°C).
- Empty contents of jar into medium mixing bowl and stir to combine ingredients.
- Beat butter and eggs in large mixing bowl.
- Add dry ingredients to egg mixture in several additions and mix well after each.
- Spread batter in sprayed 9 x 13-inch (23 x 33 cm) baking pan.
- Bake for 20 to 25 minutes or until light brown on top.
- Remove from oven and cool. Frost with Chocolate Icing while warm.

Chocolate Icing:

¼ cup (½ stick) butter	60 ml
5 tablespoons cocoa powder	75 ml
¼ cup milk	60 ml
2 cups powdered sugar	480 ml
1 teaspoon vanilla	5 ml

- Melt butter in small saucepan over low heat.
- Stir in cocoa, milk and powdered sugar and mix well.
- Remove from heat and stir in vanilla and spread over warm bars.

Frosted Butterscotch Bars

Instructions for baking:

½ cup (1 stick) butter, softened	120 ml
2 eggs	

- Preheat oven to 350° (176°C).
- Empty contents of jar into medium mixing bowl and stir to combine ingredients.
- Beat butter and eggs in large mixing bowl.
- Add dry ingredients to egg mixture in several additions and mix well after each.
- Spread batter in sprayed 9 x 13-inch (23 x 33 cm) baking pan.
- Bake for 20 to 25 minutes or until light brown on top.
- Remove from oven and cool. Frost with Chocolate Icing while warm.

Chocolate Icing:

¼ cup (½ stick) butter	60 ml
5 tablespoons cocoa powder	75 ml
¼ cup milk	60 ml
2 cups powdered sugar	480 ml
1 teaspoon vanilla	5 ml

- Melt butter in small saucepan over low heat.
- Stir in cocoa, milk and powdered sugar and mix well.
- Remove from heat and stir in vanilla and spread over warm bars.

- ✂

Frosted Butterscotch Bars

Instructions for baking:

½ cup (1 stick) butter, softened	120 ml
2 eggs	

- Preheat oven to 350° (176°C).
- Empty contents of jar into medium mixing bowl and stir to combine ingredients.
- Beat butter and eggs in large mixing bowl.
- Add dry ingredients to egg mixture in several additions and mix well after each.
- Spread batter in sprayed 9 x 13-inch (23 x 33 cm) baking pan.
- Bake for 20 to 25 minutes or until light brown on top.
- Remove from oven and cool. Frost with Chocolate Icing while warm.

Chocolate Icing:

¼ cup (½ stick) butter	60 ml
5 tablespoons cocoa powder	75 ml
¼ cup milk	60 ml
2 cups powdered sugar	480 ml
1 teaspoon vanilla	5 ml

- Melt butter in small saucepan over low heat.
- Stir in cocoa, milk and powdered sugar and mix well.
- Remove from heat and stir in vanilla and spread over warm bars.

COOKBOOKS PUBLISHED BY COOKBOOK RESOURCES, LLC

The Ultimate Cooking With 4 Ingredients
Easy Cooking With 5 Ingredients
The Best of Cooking With 3 Ingredients
Easy Gourmet-Style Cooking With 5 Ingredients
Gourmet Cooking With 5 Ingredients
Healthy Cooking With 4 Ingredients
Diabetic Cooking With 4 Ingredients
Easy Dessert Cooking With 5 Ingredients
4-Ingredient Recipes For 30-Minute Meals
Easy Slow-Cooker Cooking
Quick Fixes With Cake Mixes
Casseroles To The Rescue
Holiday Recipes
Kitchen Keepsakes/More Kitchen Keepsakes
Mother's Recipes
Recipe Keepsakes
Cookie Dough Secrets
Gifts For The Cookie Jar
Brownies In A Jar
Muffins In A Jar
Cookie Jar Magic
Quilters' Cooking Companion
Miss Sadies' Southern Cooking
Classic Tex-Mex and Texas Cooking
Classic Southwest Cooking
Classic Pennsylvania-Dutch Cooking
Classic New England Cooking
The Great Canadian Cookbook
The Best of Lone Star Legacy Cookbook
Lone Star Legacy
Lone Star Legacy II
Cookbook 25 Years
Pass The Plate
Authorized Texas Ranger Cookbook
Texas Longhorn Cookbook
Trophy Hunters' Wild Game Cookbook
Little Taste of Texas
Little Taste of Texas II
Texas Peppers
Southwest Sizzler
Southwest Ole
Class Treats
Leaving Home
Bake Sale Bestsellers
Easy Desserts

cookbook
resources LLC
Bringing Family And Friends To The Table

To Order **All New Gifts From the Cookie Jar:**

Please send_____copies @ $14.95 (U.S.) each $_____

Plus postage/handling @ $6.00 for first book $_____

and $1.00 for each additional book $_____

Texas residents add sales tax @ $ 1.20 each $_____

Check or Credit Card (Canada-credit card only)   TOTAL $_____

Charge to my   ❏ Master Card   or   ❏ Visa Card

Account #_____

Expiration Date_____

Signature_____

> Mail or Call:
> **Cookbook Resources**
> 541 Doubletree Dr.
> Highland Village, Texas 75077
> Toll Free (866) 229-2665
> (972) 317-6404 Fax
> www.cookbookresources.com

Name_____

Address_____

City_____State_____Zip_____

Phone (day)_____ (evening)_____

- -

To Order **All New Gifts From the Cookie Jar:**

Please send_____copies @ $14.95 (U.S.) each $_____

Plus postage/handling @ $6.00 for first book $_____

and $1.00 for each additional book $_____

Texas residents add sales tax @ $ 1.20 each $_____

Check or Credit Card (Canada-credit card only)   TOTAL $_____

Charge to my   ❏ Master Card   or   ❏ Visa Card

Account #_____

Expiration Date_____

Signature_____

> Mail or Call:
> **Cookbook Resources**
> 541 Doubletree Dr.
> Highland Village, Texas 75077
> Toll Free (866) 229-2665
> (972) 317-6404 Fax
> www.cookbookresources.com

Name_____

Address_____

City_____State_____Zip_____

Phone (day)_____ (evening)_____